The American
CIDER BOOK

"CIDER MAKING ON LONG ISLAND," BY WILLIAM DAVIS

The American
CIDER BOOK

The Story of America's Natural Beverage

VREST ORTON

FARRAR, STRAUS AND GIROUX   NEW YORK

To my son and business partner

Lyman K. Orton

who undertook double duty

while I took time to write

this book

Acknowledgments

Many kind souls have helped me ferret out some of the facts. Chief among them is my wife, Mildred Ellen Orton, who helped greatly with the recipes and corrected many of my assumptions about *how to cook with cider.*

Others to whom I am grateful for aid are Vivian Bryan, Vermont State Library; Marcus McCorison, curator, the American Antiquarian Society; Walter H. Hildick, president of Sterling Cider Company; Steve Martinelli, president of S. Martinelli and Co.; Colin D. Osborne, of H. F. Bulmer, Ltd., England; Professor Robert L. LaBelle, Cornell University; Robert Rodale, editor of *Organic Gardening and Farming;* and Mrs. Robert O. Frick, Pittsford, Vermont. A great deal of good information also came from Fred W. Burrows of the International Apple Institute. I received ideas from the work of Catherine Fennelly of Old Sturbridge Village, and from publications of the Society for the Preservation of New England Antiquities. Others who furnished material are mentioned in the text.

Robert Frost's poem, "In a Glass of Cider," is reprinted from *The Poetry of Robert Frost,* published by Holt, Rinehart and Winston. The two well-known paintings, *Cider Making on Long Island* by William Davis (used on the title page) and *The Cider Mill* by William T. Carlton, are reproduced here by kind permission of the New York State Historical Association, where the original paintings hang. *Cider Making,* by William Sidney Mount, is reproduced by permission of the Metropolitan Museum of New York.

Contents

IN A GLASS OF CIDER

It seemed I was a mite of sediment
That waited for the bottom to ferment
So I could catch a bubble in ascent.
I rode up on one till the bubble burst,
And when that left me to sink back reversed
I was no worse off than I was at first.
I'd catch another bubble if I waited.
The thing was to get now and then elated.

Robert Frost

The American
CIDER BOOK

Introduction

In the last part of his life, which ended so tragically, Ernest Hemingway undertook a rugged and exhausting safari into the wilds of Africa. He was always one to test strength to the breaking point, but this journey, while it did that very thing, was designed to track down a lion his wife Mary could shoot. There was something of mystic significance about Miss Mary getting a lion.

In telling about the safari Hemingway begins to grow nostalgic about his boyhood in Michigan, because his favorite drink in the hot African night was Bulmer's Dry Cider. This beverage triggered memories of the old cider mills he knew as a young man.

It also triggered a few memories of my own, since Hemingway and I were contemporaries and from time to time had run across each other in New York and especially in Paris. The happy times when we and other American expatriates hung out at the Rotonde, the Dôme, and other such watering places in the twenties came back into my mind and my heart. And these recollections triggered memories even more remote in time to the far-off and happy days when, as a small boy in northern Vermont, I would ride with my grandfather on the seat of a lumber wagon full of apples to be fetched to the cider mill, from where later they would come back as potable cider and, eventually, vinegar.

Hemingway, Paris, youth, and cider. More than this you don't need!

Since all but one are now out of my reach, a look at cider seemed imperative. It took me two years, off and on, to find out what I wanted to know. I discovered, much to my surprise, that while there are today in print the expected U.S. Department of Agriculture bureaucratic-language brochures on making cider on the farm, and while there are in libraries several books on cider, most are about English or French cider making, none is recent, and all are out of print.

I found no single volume covering both the history of American cider and ways to make cider today, and especially ways to use it in cooking. Many of us who live in rural New England still buy a 36-gallon keg of sweet cider in the fall, let it ferment, and then bottle it, with a smidgen of sugar in each bottle, and come up with what the French call champagne cider and what we call sparkling cider—a rousing good drink.

Especially intriguing and, I discovered, almost completely forgotten was the custom in America (which still exists in the back country) of using cider in cooking, as the French use wine.

These were, I thought, good enough reasons for a book on the subject of cider. But in the months of research and organizing the rich material that it was my good fortune to discover about cider, I learned a great deal.

In the course of my work I have formulated three definite opinions on cider making.

First: In spite of the long, well-documented, and fruitful history of how cider has been made in this country for at least three hundred years, and in spite of the many improvements consistently introduced into this noble art, there still exist in rural regions some cider makers who have learned nothing and who continue to turn out a juice which is supposed to be cider but which is made from rotten, wormy, and often dirty apples.

Second: I am now convinced that my mother's and my wife's stern policy, demonstrated in their homes, that "cleanliness is next to Godliness" is not farfetched when it comes to making cider. There is no reason whatsoever why good, clean, pure, delectable cider cannot be made using the same stern respect for cleanliness, with equal amounts of logic or common sense. That you can produce something good from something bad is, I suspect, believed today by some cider makers, and demonstrated by none.

Third: The author of this book has no Messianic complex. He harbors no intent to change and assuredly no hope of changing the slovenly habits of people who are content with their own practices. But I hope that any reader who is intrigued with the wonderful history of America's outstanding natural beverage, good American cider, hard or sweet, will want to discover how and why it was made and ought to be made and that, with a bit of patience, care, and work, as well as luck, it can be made by himself. This, I think, is another reason for this book.

Beer-sipping Babylonian courtiers, circa 1900 B.C.

1

A Short History of Cider

*T*here are three natural intoxicating beverages as old as man: wine, beer, and cider. No one doubts the antiquity of beer or wine, which were made from almost any grain, fruit, vegetable, or plant. The Egyptians were making a form of beer, called barley wine, as early as 5000 B.C. Most ancient peoples brewed beer and wine long before the Christian era.* More recently, in New England, beer was concocted of such strange things as sap from the sugar-maple tree, and wine was brewed from wild dandelion greens.

Since cider had to be made from apples, however, and apples could be grown only in the temperate zones, cider was less known worldwide and came into common use only at a later date.

Just how late such a date is becomes difficult to determine. We know that in the year 55 B.C., Julius Caesar led two Roman legions to Kent, England, and that eventually the Romans penetrated into the heart of the island. Even then, at least fifty years before the birth of Christ, the Romans found cider to be a common drink. Celtic mythology tells us that the apple was a sacred fruit; an apple god was worshipped by the primitive tribes of England. Even while centuries of darkness lay heavy upon this

* See my *Homemade Beer Book.*

island, the first cider was made from the earliest-known apples—
wild apples that we know today as crab apples. In some places
such as France, crab-apple cider (verjuice) is still prized as a
rare, and probably very tart, drink. It is certain that all cultivated
apples sprang from the wild crab, so it is correct to say that the
rough beverage of that dim far-off era was the progenitor of our
present drinkable cider.

In the year of Our Lord 77, Pliny the Elder, in his famous
natural history, mentions a drink made from the natural juice of
apples. In the third century, cider was known and drunk in
Europe. In the fourth century, St. Jerome used the term *sicera* for
drinks made from apples, and from this word came our name
cider. In France, Charlemagne enforced laws to promote and control the proper manufacture of cider.

One French authority (G. Warcollier) declares that in the
eleventh and twelfth centuries, cider was more popular than
beer. By the eighteenth century, more scientific methods had
been devised for the manufacture of cider in Europe and treatises
began to appear on cider making. These helped spread the word
and increased the popularity of the beverage. One rather surprising fact emerges from Monsieur Warcollier's many statistics:
as late as 1940, the annual production of cider in France, the
greatest wine-producing nation in the world, was 260 million gallons, while only 900 million gallons of wine were produced in
the same period. France has the largest acreage of land devoted
to cider apples of any nation in the old world. A devotee of
Hemingway or one who has traveled extensively in France will
be well aware of the noble taste of Calvados, the cider brandy
that Normandy is famous for.

A noted French authority on wines, in a treatise published well
over a hundred fifty years ago, set forth the theory that Normandy
became the leading French region for apple culture, and hence
cider, because, as he expressed it, "I know very few people who
have tasted the wines, even the most renowned ones, of lower
Normandy. These few people declare unanimously that such
Normandy wines were absolutely undrinkable."

Cider making can certainly be traced to the primitive tribes of

Gaul. A celebrated tapestry, woven before the age of William the Conqueror, depicts barrels of cider. Certainly, the writer Oliver Basselin was giving cider an accolade when in 1550 he praised "the sweet juice of the apple tree." As early as 1573, a man named Gaulmier gave the world a famous *Traité du Sidre*. While several hundred years ago it was generally acknowledged that the best cider in the world came from the region of Contentin, cider probably originated in the Basque country of northwest Spain. It is recorded in *Traité du Sidre* that a Spaniard with the odd name of Dursus de l'Etre brought apple trees into France in 1486. Looking at more modern statistics, it has been estimated that about a hundred years ago there were 4,290,000 apple trees in France. All the cider made in France in one year, if poured into a dry lake bed, would occupy nearly a hundred acres and be at least one meter deep. Although over the centuries many French writers have been displeased with the quality of cider, having as they did fine wines for comparison, all agreed that cider was a healthy, nourishing beverage and good for mankind.

Some interesting comments on the rich history of cider in England come from England's famous cider company. H. P. Bulmer, Ltd., which made the dry cider that Ernest Hemingway relished. Bulmer's was founded in 1887 (the year of Queen Victoria's Jubilee) and the Royal Warrant was conferred on this establishment in 1911. With their two thousand acres of apple trees, supplemented by the produce of some three hundred private apple growers, Bulmer's is today the largest cider-making concern in the world. Its storage tank, the world's greatest, holds 1,100,000 gallons of cider. With these distinctions, it is not surprising that Bulmer's has issued a fascinating story of cider making in England. The following excerpt is pertinent:

"Cider has continued to give pleasure in every age. In the early Middle Ages, for example, there are many references in monastic writings to cider, a drink evidently much enjoyed by the monks. It was also clearly popular in the 14th century as William of Shoreham reflected the Church's concern for the niceties of sacramental rites by stating that young children were not to be baptised with cider! William Langdon refers to it in *Piers Plowman* and Shakespeare in *A Midsummer Night's Dream*.

Cider became a welcome substitute for French wine during the Hundred Years' War when supplies of the latter were cut off, although its popularity was not always universal: Eleanor de Montfort (wife of Simon) has recorded that it was a less fashionable drink among the members of the baronial class of her time. Daniel Defoe observed that Hereford people 'boaft the richeft cider in all Britain' and Samuel Pepys notes in his diary (for what the information is worth) that he, on 1st May, 1666, 'drank a cup of Syder.' From the 17th century much verse was written on the subject of cider, praising it in poems of varying literary merit both as an aid to good cheer and as a homely cure for almost every ailment known to man.

"In England, apples such as Hangdown's, Skyrum's Kerne, Old Foxwhelp, Slack-my-Girdle, Golden Ball, Handsome Mand's, Ruby Streak, Yellow Styres, Golden Pippins, Woodbines Duckbill, Cats' Heads, Sheep's Nose, Lady's Finger once went into the making of cider. These cider apples with such romantic and unusual names—there are over 350 different known varieties—were locally grown in the past. Perhaps more than to any other man we owe their classification and development to a courtier of Charles I who retired to his estate at Holme Lacy where he devoted his life to the cultivation of cider apples. To this day Herefordshire cider drinkers still raise their glasses to Lord Scudamore; but particularly they are raised by the Bulmer family who have put the results of his efforts to such good use. The cider apples of today still retain that special bloom, richness and character that make Herefordshire cider such a distinctive drink.

"Herefordshire orchards are a glorious sight in springtime when all the blossom is out—but the really hard work of harvesting and cider making comes in the autumn. The season for cider making begins slowly, usually in mid-September, and then builds up to a peak in October and November. The tree is shaken, the ripe apple falls and is gathered from the soft grass into lorry, truck and trailer for immediate delivery to the factory. The apples are graded on arrival and then tipped into vast concrete pits known as silos. Along these silos run streams of water which wash the apples as they rush along to the mills. The apples are raised into the press house and, after passing through a rotary drum for a final wash and polish, are reduced to pulp. This pulp is spread on coarse cloth in layers, one on top of the other, until a pile of about four feet high is prepared. A hydraulic press squeezes and the juice gushes out. It rests in settling vats adjoining the vat house before being pumped to the storage vats for fermentation. This commences at once and is caused by the action of the yeast

which is present on the outer skin of the apples. Fermentation continues until the sugar has been converted into alcohol and carbonic acid gas. The resulting liquid is a very dry cider."

In England, up to the twentieth century, hard cider was a popular rural drink. It was cheaper than beer, and since it was about 7% alcohol, country cider was as potent as most beers. Every farmer made cider for his family and help, and the landed gentry owned large cider presses to furnish their tenants with plenty of cider for a working day. Country dwellers who had given up making cider and those who had never possessed a cider press availed themselves of a traveling cider press that was hauled by horse from house to house and pressed cider from any apples the farmer could gather and have ready. One English commentator made a wild guess that 20 million gallons of cider were made each year by home methods, equaling or perhaps surpassing the 20 million gallons known to have been produced by commercial cider manufacturers.

Since the average apple contains as much as 80% juice, cider is made any place on the globe where apples thrive. The principal cider-producing regions are France, England, Holland, and the United States. In England in the eighteenth century about two thousand varieties of apples were grown, and in 1850 in the United States one authority on horticulture listed a thousand different strains.

The mid-nineteenth century was a high point; apple raising and cider making reached a peak in the United States, because agriculture was the principal occupation of the great majority (75%) of Americans. It is interesting to take a look at the names of that era's most popular apples, a good mixture of which made the best cider. Among the best known "summer apples" used to give aroma to the blend were Pearman, Red Astrachan, Benoni, Bevan's Favorite, Bohanan, Caroline Red June, Early Harvest, Early Strawberry, Early Joe, Garretson's Early, Golden Sweet, Keswick Codlin, Lyman's Pumpkin Sweet, Manomet, Oslin, Summer Belle-fleur, Sweet Paradise, Summer Rose, Summer Queen, Sops of Wine, and William's Favorite.

The "fall apples" were Emperor Alexander, Autumn Swaar, Beauty of Kent, Bailey Spice, Clyde Beauty, Duchess of Oldenburg, Cloth of Gold, Fall Pippin, Fleiner, Garden Royal, Sassafras Sweet Cole, Jewett's Fine Red, Queen Anne, Maiden's Blush,

A good example of the apple grinder used on farms about a hundred years ago to make pomace

Lyman's Pound Sweet, Porter, Pomme Royal, President, Spice Sweet, Smoke-House, Tomkins, and Sweet Paradise.

The "winter apples" had equally delightful names, such as Siberian Crab, Flowering Chinese, Bourrassa, Bell-Flower, Belle et Bonne, Carthouse, Dominie, Fameuse, Fallawater, Fort Miami, King, Jonathan, Limber Twig, Mother, Pomme d'Api, Minister, Ortley, Peck's Pleasant, Pickman, Pryor's Red, Rawle's Jannet, Russet Golden, Seek-No-Further, Winter Blush, Winesap, and Wine Apple.

In writing about cider, Henry Ward Beecher, the most celebrated American clergyman of the age, declared in 1859 that ". . . there is a pleasure in having a decorous name to a good fruit." We certainly agree with the reverend doctor that these and countless other charming names placed on apples "made the mouth water." Dr. Beecher commented that Demoiselle, Lady's Flesh, and Love's Pear were "very proper for young lovers." He mentions other names of apples that make you wonder about their origin—names such as Burnt Cat, Priest's Pear, Trout Pear, Sheep-nose, and Leathercoat. The Russet apple, the size, color, and taste of which I can still remember after fifty years, was well thought of in Dr. Beecher's time. He quotes one large orchardist in Belfe, Ohio, who, on being asked for a list of the best apple varieties for an orchard of a thousand trees, said: "Take 999 Golden Russets and the rest you can choose for yourself." Dr. Beecher describes the Russet as strong, upright, admirable, healthy, spicy, very juicy, and tender. Considering all this praise, it is unfortunate that one can seldom find the variety today.

The reason I dwell at length on the subject of apples, their names, and their widespread cultivation a hundred years back, is that now that cider has come into its own and won a new popularity as a natural American drink, I hope the pomologists will be inspired to restore interest in and cultivation of some of the wonderful old-time apples that have been forgotten. There are so many! Even as late as the 1870's P. Barry, in his book *Barry's Fruit Garden*, noted that in the twenty years since 1850 there had been a great increase in new varieties of apples. He estimated that there were no less than four thousand strains under cultivation! Each section of the country had its own unique ones. Anyone who has explored the back-beyond regions of New England can vouch for Mr. Barry's comments on the venerable age apple trees can achieve. He mentions that (in 1870) there was still visible in Rhode Island the stump of an apple tree that had been planted in 1748. Near it was a new greening that had sprung from the ancient mother tree.

Although apples (and cider) have added zest and legend to American history, the apple as we know it was not indigenous to the North American continent.* The Indians gave the Pilgrims corn, a historic and truly indigenous American product, but there is no mention of apples until apple seeds were included among supplies stored in ships bringing colonists to this land in the seventeenth century. The fact that the hardy English adventurers in their journey into the wilderness of New England had the forethought to take along apple seeds is proof that they intended to stay. The first New England native was Peregrine White, born on the *Mayflower* ship as it lay in the harbor on November 20, 1620. The record states that when this lad grew up he planted apple seeds. Another and later planter of apple seeds was John Chapman, who became a subject of folk song and story as Johnny Appleseed. He gave the region beyond the Alleghenies its first apples, and its first cider.

New England legend and history are rich in references to apples. Only nine years after the landing at Plymouth, apple trees were being planted in the Massachusetts Bay Colony. One early history records that in 1638, at a spot at the foot of what is now Beacon Hill in Boston, a man named Blaxton grew apple trees. When Harvard was only a mewling infant, there were several apple orchards in Boston and cider was stored in every cellar. Because the early apple crop of Massachusetts Bay Colony had not then been perfected into sweet, juicy, eating apples, most of the crop was used for cider.

* Small crab apples are known to have existed in the North American continent before the arrival of the white man, but they were highly astringent and were only edible after considerable cooking. There is no evidence that these indigenous American crab apples were ever used by the Indians to make cider.

About seventy-five years ago, the Encyclopaedia Britannica listed sixty of the most popular varieties of apples grown in England. As footnote to the source of our American apples, it is interesting that the following apples, so familiar to us in the United States today, were listed as indigenous to England: Astrachan, Pippin, Russet, Northern Spy, Gravenstein, and Greening.

It is hard for us, the almost completely urbanized Americans of today, to realize how widespread the use of cider was in early New England. The early settlers had tea, as well as coffee and chocolate, as every student of New England knows. But cider was the natural country drink, readily, easily, and cheaply made from the farmers' own apples and drunk by every member of the family, including women, children, and hired hands. Actually, cider was cheaper than beer. One historian reports that, in 1767, 1.14 barrels of cider per capita were drunk in Massachusetts! Catherine Fennelly in her book *Food, Drink, and Recipes of Early New England,* published by Old Sturbridge Village, notes that respectable women and children would not drink the whiskey and beer openly sold

at distilleries and breweries, even though it cost only 25 cents a gallon, with the earthenware jug thrown in. Instead, they paid 28 cents a gallon, and provided their own container, for the privilege of drinking at home. Therefore, cost was one reason for the prevalence of cider as the typical New England family drink.

The low cost of cider and its immediate availability could not, however, have been the reason why John Adams, our second President, drank a tankard of hard cider every morning before breakfast until the end of his life. President Adams lived to be ninety-one years old. Cider was generally drunk in the country houses for breakfast and by travelers at inns and taverns. College students were commonly served cider with all meals. An early president of Harvard College (Mr. Holyoke) noted in his diary (1743 to 1759) that he had put down sixteen barrels of cider one fall, and a few years later he thought it important to record that he went back to the cellar and added spirits to thirteen barrels of hard cider to give it greater authority.

When the New England farmer made cider in the fall, it went into large wooden barrels for "working." If he was going to do the proper thing, he would lay down at least ten barrels of hard cider on the cold earth floor of his cellar—enough to last out the long winter months.

There is no doubt that the consumption of cider in the nineteenth century reached such a high level that concerned do-gooders raised the specter of temperance. In 1874 the National Women's Christian Temperance Union was formed. However, from 1870 to 1892 the consumption of alcoholic beverages in the United States rose from about seven and a half gallons to seventeen gallons per capita!

When sailing ships went out from New England ports, the ships' stores of flour, potatoes, and salted meat were enhanced by an adequate supply of hard cider. The fact that cider was freely consumed at house and barn raisings and at military musters is almost too well known for comment. When a farm was offered for sale, the owner took pains to mention that among the principal assets was a cider mill. Most of the agricultural fairs set up prizes for the best cider but made it clear that adequate samples for testing must be furnished—at least ten gallons.

Cider as a political tool reached its apotheosis in the great campaign of 1840 when the Whigs nominated General William Henry Harrison for President and John Tyler for Vice President. At that convention, cider was very much in evidence. The Vermont delegation made itself nationally known at the convention when all seven delegates carried a banner with the prophetic words, "THE GREEN MOUNTAIN BOYS WILL DO THEIR OWN VOTING AND THEIR OWN FIGHTING." The national slogan of what later became the Republican Party was "Tippecanoe and Tyler Too." To publicize Harrison's humble origins (he had been born in a log cabin, where, certainly, the daily beverage was hard cider), the prominent symbol of all political gatherings in this campaign was a barrel of cider. Even campaign headquarters was housed in a log cabin with a barrel of cider out front. Cider was served free to all who could or would vote.

The campaign was the most spectacular waged in the nation up to that time. In Vermont it created a legend and a historic site that have survived to this day. The peak of the campaign in Vermont came on July 8, 1840. Daniel Webster, the greatest orator of the day (and perhaps of any day), did not have time to deliver three speeches in three different parts of New England, so he elected to deliver only one. The spot was determined by geometric triangulation of the three points. It turned out to be a wild mountainside in the high, remote southern Vermont township of Stratton—a place described in a contemporary account as "far from the haunts of men, scarcely a house being visible." (The same can be said today.) The amazing fact is that an estimated ten thousand persons made the long journey by horse-drawn vehicle up long, narrow, twisting dirt roads to this forest summit to hear the great Webster speak. This story is now engraved on a historic-sites marker in this still wild part of Vermont. However, the marker does not mention that every wagon had at least one jug of hard cider under the seat. What the horses drank is not recorded either. The results of "the cider campaign" are interesting. Vermont gave the largest majority to the Harrison-Tyler, log-cabin-and-cider ticket, in proportion to votes cast, of any state in the Union. General Harrison won the Presidency by an electoral landslide vote of 234 to 60.

Historical records about cider reveal how close cider was to the everyday life of the rural folk of the nineteenth century, especially in New England. By this I mean not only its availability as a daily beverage but also its home manufacture. Cider presses were so natural a part of the New England landscape that one could not go very far in farming country without coming upon one. They were, of course, homemade. I recall, from my boyhood in northern Vermont, several such mills, with massive wood screws and the long pole for hitching the horse which did the work of turning the screw to press the apples into cider.

So integral a part of New England folklore was cider that Currier and Ives issued a hand-colored lithograph, after a painting by Durrie, showing cider making on a New England farm. It was one of their most popular prints.

While cider mills were probably not as numerous as cheese factories, which at one time numbered over two hundred and fifty in Vermont, certainly there were few rural towns in this state that did not have a cider mill, so farmers would not be obliged to drive the lumber wagon far to have their apples made into cider.

In the age of the horse, cider mills had the same geographical reason for being as did cheese and butter factories. It is difficult to realize today that a hundred years ago the great majority of New Englanders were rural people living in small villages or on self-supporting farms. Even in my boyhood (not quite *that* long ago), where my grandfather and later my father ran a country store in a small, remote Vermont country town, the inhabitants never dreamed of going to the store to buy vinegar any more than they would to buy maple syrup, a peck of apples or potatoes, or any other produce indigenous to the region. The man whose winter cellar was not stored with barrels of vinegar, several barrels of good winter apples, mason jars of apple butter and applesauce

on the dark cool shelves, big 25-gallon earthenware crocks of cucumber pickles, eggs in water glass, and salt pork in tangy brine, as well as home-cured, cob-smoked hams, would have been considered a wastrel and run out of town.

So I like to think about cider, not just for its wonderful taste, but because it was so typical of frugal New England folk, who used what they had, made do with what they could raise, and considered it a lifelong disgrace (even unto the next generation) to call on the town for help (today known as "welfare").

Yes, cider was a great drink: either sweet cider or hard cider. Up to the year 1930, more cider was made and drunk than any other fruit juice. Soon after this date, when Florida and California entrepreneurs began to sell the nation orange juice, cider (though it contained as much ascorbic acid, Vitamin C, as citrus juices and was cheaper) was relegated to nostalgic occasions such as Thanksgiving and Halloween.

Today all this has changed.

The day of natural foods and drinks has dawned. The seeds that such pioneers as J. R. Rodale and, today, his son Bob planted years ago have borne fruit. Not only are millions of Americans eating and drinking natural foods and beverages (uncontaminated by adulteration, processing, and additives), but hundreds of thousands are going to the land, either in a small kitchen-garden way or with a real farming enterprise.

Cider is a natural drink. Unlike orange juice, its main ingredient can be grown all over the United States in a small way for family consumption. The cider itself can be made without costly equipment, great investment, or too great scientific knowledge.

And it should be!

2

General Methods of Cider Making

OLD-TIME PRINCIPLES

*I*f there had been over the years one simple, agreed-upon method of making cider, there would be no need for this chapter.

That American cider has been concocted in so many different ways is what makes the subject as fascinating as it is complex. As a matter of fact, cider (unlike man) *is* capable of perfection, and as with wine, each method has its devotees. Yet it would be irreverent to write a book praising the first four growths of the great French wines of Bordeaux (and such books have been written) and then give equal coverage to the charming amateur attempts by little old ladies in remote farmhouses to make and lay down a few bottles of dandelion wine. The perfection that the noble wines of France have achieved in their vintage years, due to soil, climate, painstaking care, and God's grace, is one story. The concoction of homemade wines from native fruits and other growing things of field and woods is another.

The same can be said about cider.

The perfection that cider can reach, by proper scientific

methods, great care, and much time either in the home or in commercial enterprises, is one story. But first we shall tell the story of how cider was made (especially in New England, where it has its greatest history) by the average farmer, using his own apples and his own hand-built cider press, which was as much a part of farm equipment in the nineteenth century as the bull rake, the hickory handle of a scythe, or the hayrack on the lumber wagon.

The Society for the Preservation of New England Antiquities thought well enough of this subject and the signal importance of cider to the history of folkways of this part of the world that it devoted several pages in one of its publications, written by Ruth Howard Allen, to how cider was made years ago in rural New England.

Farm magazines of the nineteenth century consistently devoted several pages to cider-making methods and published strong editorials urging farmers to pay more attention to the quality of cider. These critics felt, with good reason, that the harsh and crude cider produced by careless farmers in the late eighteenth and the first quarter of the nineteenth century could be improved. One writer in 1824 emphasized that the manufacture of cider on the farms was the worst managed of any agricultural procedure. He tried to shame New England farmers into better efforts by citing the fact that the Shakers of Canterbury, New Hampshire, were making such fine cider that it was in constant demand by faraway Bostonians, who were willing to pay as much as $10 a barrel for this superior vintage. Surprisingly enough, at the same time New Jersey farmers were also making a quality cider so good that they were shipping it to the West Indies and even to Europe. This was as good a trick as carrying coals to Newcastle.

A good word for the farmers of Bergen County, New Jersey, and Rockland County, New York (neighbors on the border), is put in here because my memory goes back to the twenties. During those dark ages when the Eighteenth Amendment, the Volstead Act, was wreaking havoc in this nation, I lived in New York City. To avoid the dangers of bathtub gin and other virulent concoctions made by the bootleggers of Manhattan, those of us in the know who retained a sensitive palate crossed the Hudson River to Bergen or Rockland County and fetched back gallon jugs of good, sound, well-made, and highly potable applejack—the state in which cider reaches ultimate perfection. Farmers west of the Hudson did not bother to sell sweet or hard cider, bottled cider, or any other kind of cider. They distilled all the hard cider into cider brandy, then known as applejack. This safe, wholesome, natural beverage probably saved more lives and promoted more temperance than all the efforts of the Women's Christian Temperance Union or the official federal enforcers of the Volstead Act.

True temperance was the desire of all well-tempered men of good will at that time, and cider was their drink. But the good man's well-meaning efforts at temperance were often foiled by the misguided radical abstainers. Like bachelors who recoil from connubiality because of their total ignorance of this blessed state, such do-gooders knew nothing about the drinking habits of mankind. It was these jealous and zealous abstainers who forced the Prohibition law upon the United States. In the early 1930's, when the Eighteenth Amendment was fortunately repealed, such bleeding hearts seized political power in many state legislatures. Because of their total ignorance of drinking customs, they were able to get laws passed governing the sale and use of liquor that achieved not temperance but just the opposite.* State

* For example, one early regulation of the Vermont state liquor control law forbade drinkers from standing at a bar to imbibe. In accordance with the law, customers had to sit down and have the drinks brought them. Everybody who ever took a drink of the mildest form knows that a person can drink a great deal more sitting down than standing up, and usually does. The word *sotted* means not only a fool but a drunk too far gone to stand.

liquor commissions have been struggling with these absurd, un-realistic, early-1930 laws ever since, and the burden is a ridiculous one indeed.

Cider was, and still is, a temperance drink. It was commonly served at all family occasions and at festive celebrations such as weddings, christenings, Thanksgiving, and Halloween. Even devoted pillars of the church, as well as most clergy and deacons, laid down barrels of cider against the winter evenings. These gentlemen would have recoiled in horror from strong drink. I remember that as a boy in northern Vermont I was not at all sur-prised to see my uncle (who *was* a deacon in the Baptist church and a good man) go down cellar in the mid-evening after supper and bring up a tin pan of apples along with a pitcher of foaming cider, both of which he consumed as he sat in front of the kitchen stove. Had he gone into a saloon and imbibed whiskey or rum, the family would have been shocked beyond measure.

Being a family affair, cider also has its superstitions—especially in its making. Many cider makers held firm notions about the re-lation between cider making and the weather. The best cider, they thought, was made when the wind was blowing from the west or northwest. When the wind was blowing from the south, cider would have an unpleasant taste. One Massachusetts farmer re-ported that cider made when the wind was from the northwest was of a rich color and a finer drink.

There was much disagreement about the apples from which cider could be made. Slovenly farmers made a slipshod product by shoveling into a wagon all the rotten, dirty, wormy apples that had fallen under the trees, and then driving this garbage to the cider mill. To such persons, cider was a by-product, made of by-products. One comment of those early days is pertinent: "The practice of considering cider as something made from rotten apples, or apples that are not good for anything else, is a shocking insult to the art of cider making."

Many treatises from about a hundred years ago reiterated the opinion that very few farmers knew how to make good cider. One declared that apples not perfectly sound and well ripened were not fit for cider and that, to prevent bruising, apples should always be hand-picked (a far cry from shoveling up the debris of the orchard). Such perfectionists held that all apples should be examined and blemishes cut out, and then each apple should be washed and wiped dry.

In spite of the well-known fact that most farmers made cider with whole apples, and often off-grade apples, an encyclopedia compiled sixty years ago not only advocated coring cider apples before grinding them into pomace, but described a special machine designed for quick coring. It was based on the simple principle that today is used by the housewife who plunges a round, stainless-steel gadget down through the center of the apple to remove the core. The machine in this compendium was activated by a spring and was built into a table. The chief reason for removing the core before making cider was to avoid crushing the apple seeds and thus imparting a bitter taste to the resulting juice.

There was a saying that any farmer who disdained cider was a man who exhibited not a horror of strong drink but a horror of drinking the foul stuff he produced. Some farmers fell into neither camp and used cider only to produce vinegar which their wives used in cooking.

What Is Cider?

There are still a great many opinions about cider, and such views vary from definite to contradictory, from highly prejudiced to middle-of-the-road. This, about a subject so American as cider, is as it should be.

What cider is, even today, remains a moot question in scientific circles. Leigh P. Beadle, author of the well-known book *Brew It Yourself,* can be cited as a typical holder of emphatic views concerning cider. Mr. Beadle declares:

"It is appalling to me that people will pay $1.25 for a jug of *sweet* apple cider and then drink it up before it has been blessed by the kiss of the yeast. Apple cider in its unfermented state ranks with the kiddie drinks and other assorted beverages that fill the grocer's shelves. Add a little brewers' yeast or wine yeast to apple cider and you have an entirely different drink. The resulting beverage is delicious, refreshing, slightly carbonated, and even a little alcoholic. It is now in its 'natural' state, and all the good things of life are better in their natural state."

Now, there are some who would cavil at Mr. Beadle's forthright definitions, especially these days when the word "natural" is overworked by many far-out food faddists. It is true that the clean, delectable sweet juice which gushes out of the cider press from good cider apples is about as "natural" a drink as you can get. But, if left alone for a spell, nature takes its relentless course, and one day, after the "natural" process of fermentation takes place, you'll have hard cider that contains alcohol. This is perfectly *natural* too!

It is no wonder that there is confusion today about cider, apple juice, and the alcoholic drink into which sweet cider can turn.

"There's no substitute for the old screw press and fresh, untreated cider," declares Robert L. LaBelle, Professor of Food Science at Cornell's State Agriculture Experiment Station at Geneva, New York. Dr. LaBelle has published a number of interesting papers on apple cider which are of decided value to today's cider makers. In a 1971 monograph he states: "In my opinion . . . the term *fresh, sweet or farm* cider should be reserved to the simple old-fashioned product, normally oxidized in color and flavor and still containing all the suspended solids that render it almost opaque . . . However, all processing, such as heating or the addition of ascorbic acid that largely prevents oxidation, produces 'apple juice,' *not* cider."

In an interview with Professor LaBelle in the Syracuse (N.Y.) *Herald American,* Richard H. Case gives us a charming description of sweet cider being made. Mr. Case declares that in pressing cider apples on a New York farm ". . . there is joy in watching a few drops of the amber juice fall into the pan. And

some satisfaction that you have squeezed your own apples into a jug of additiveless 'country cider.' With a velvety hiss, a pure white stream plunged into the pitcher. Then it went silent as foam built up like cotton. A mellow, fruity aroma floated out . . . This mellow aroma is still with us . . ." Mr. Case then quotes a New York farmer on the subject. "The only way to have real cider is just as it comes from the press. When you start putting things in to preserve it, you spoil the flavor."

In this country that's the real definition of *sweet cider;* if it is permitted to ferment and produce alcohol, it's *hard cider.* Treated and canned or hermetically sealed immediately after it comes from the press, it's *apple juice.*

This confusion as to what is and what is not cider is principally the fault of cider makers, who often don't know the proper terms themselves. Of course, this may be part of a national confusion due to an ignorance of semantics, but I suspect that cider makers' ignorance is deeper than the true meaning of terms. For example, as I was finishing this book, I picked up a newspaper in which a cider maker was featured as one of the biggest producers in the Eastern United States. He had declared that ". . . our cider is pasteurized and vacuum packed at 200° F. because it must have shelf life." This man should be informed that he is not turning out *cider* but *apple juice.* There is nothing wrong with apple juice, even though it has little taste and most assuredly little taste of apples, as does pure natural sweet cider. But heating sweet cider to 200° F. kills living organisms that, if left to do their natural work, will turn sweet cider into hard cider. What is worse, such high heat kills the natural flavor and gives the liquid what I can only describe as a "cooked" taste.

So, when you buy cider from a roadside stand or from a store, be sure to ascertain, if you can, whether it is untreated, unpasteurized sweet cider, or whether it has been treated and turned into apple juice.

The confusion in the public mind about these terms is also due to the fact that in Europe, with a history of centuries of cider making, the word *cider* means fermented juice with an alcoholic content—what we call *hard* cider.

Since this book is intended to celebrate American cider, we shall use only the two terms *sweet cider* and *hard cider.*

Cider Apples

During the nineteenth century there were countless recipes for blending apples to make good cider. It was generally agreed that a blend of more than one variety made better cider than one kind alone. A 150-year-old record declared that the best cider came from a mash of the finest ripe, sound Pippin *and* crab apples. Another said cider should come only from an equal mixture of sweet apples and what they called sour apples. One cider maker known to me would often utter firm opinions on the kind of apples to be used—he preferred Northern Spy, Greenings, and Baldwins, the tarter the better. He would like to have used Russets, which he considered the best, but this rare, brown-skin variety has nearly died out.

Since the flavor of the cider was the only reason for blending, apples were selected because of their high sugar and acid content. Both properties were determined by tasting the apples rather than (as in recent times) by scientific tests. By rule of thumb and something that has, in today's computerized world, gone out of style (I refer to human judgment), the old-fashioned farmer managed to come up with a good balance between acidity and sweetness. He produced a drink that suggested the aromatic and good, fresh taste of McIntosh apples.

In apples there is indeed a wide latitude of taste. Apples vary from 6% to 20% in sugar and in acid from 1/10 of one percent to over one percent. Considering this wide variation, it is highly possible that the old-time rule of thumb employed by the New England farmer was a pretty good rule for choosing apples. In spite of what was known about blending, most farmers used the apples they raised, and any farmer fastidious enough to search the countryside for apples different from his own would have been suspect.

Making Pomace with a Stone

Since cider could not be extracted of whole apples, the apples were ground or mashed into a pulp or mash called *pomace*. This was something like coarse applesauce, except that it was uncooked and contained skins, core, and seeds mixed together.

The first apparatus devised to do this job, the "stone wheel," as the farmers called it, was related to the old stone mills used to grind grain. The apples were shoveled into a large circular trough and the heavy stone wheel ran over the apples. The wheel

"Cider Making" by William Sidney Mount

was turned by a horse hitched to the end of a long, stout pole. With a halter and rope, the horse would continue to go around the circle until the apples were crushed to a pulp inside the trough.

No farmers bothered or had the time in those days to core the apples to remove the seeds. A few authorities claimed that apple seeds tainted the juice and that the perfect cider could not be made with seeds in the pomace. One even invented a machine to extract the seeds, but it was never widely used. Most farmers, if they ever gave it thought, felt that the seeds did no harm, because the pressing did not crush them.

Grinding the apples into pulp was usually accomplished at night. The mash was then let stand, to give the pomace a darker color. Today the process is called oxidation.

The Cider Press of Early Days

The old-fashioned cider press was a simple, easy-to-understand machine, usually made by the farmer himself from hand-hewn, 10-inch beams, like those used to build houses or barns, and a massive wood screw. Some presses had one screw; others, two. At the bottom of each screw was an opening for inserting a stout pole or lever. The threaded top part of each screw turned inside a threaded hole in the big crossbeam of the frame.

Turning these massive screws (6 to 8 inches in diameter) was often accomplished by sheer manual strength. It is difficult for people today to comprehend how in those days men could exert such tremendous physical energy. Most farmers had to. Some, however, made a horse do the work. Instead of a hand-operated lever, a long pole was inserted into the hole of the screw, and a horse walked around and around the press. The pressure was exerted on the apple pomace from the top by a thick, heavy wood platform with a series of pressboards lowered inch by inch as the screws were turned.

First the pomace had to be laid into the press. A thick layer of clean rye straw was put on the floor of the press. On top of this was placed a square or oblong wood frame four inches deep. The pomace was shoveled inside this frame with a wood shovel and leveled off even with the top of the frame. The next step was to take away the frame and fold the straw around the four sides of the layer of pomace so, when pressure was applied, it would not squirt out of the press. This laying down of sections of apple pomace was repeated, laying each section of pomace at right angles to the first, until as many as a dozen were piled up in the press to make the "cheese." Between each layer of pomace it was necessary to insert a layer of wood slats called pressboards.

Now heavy wood planks were laid on top of the "cheese" to form a platform and this was lowered until the pressure slowly squeezed out the juice. From between the pressboards atop each layer of pomace the cider trickled down into a trough or channel cut into the wooden platform on which the cheese rested and then ran through a groove into an open tub. This was sweet cider.

Not all the juice could be obtained at the first pressing, so the straw was removed and another "cheese" built up using the same pomace. This time the pomace was cut (as cheese is cheddared) with a long, heavy knife. Finally, the last drop of cider was obtained and the pomace was given to pigs, who relished it. Nothing was wasted.

All manner of changes and some improvements were later invented to make cider more quickly and economically and, sometimes, better. But the general principle remained the same. All a man had to do was get all the juice out of all the apples.

Although cider made "country style" in later times was strained through clean layers of cheesecloth before barreling, early New England farmers swore by the method of straining through coarse sand from the bottom of a stream or pond. Others used flannel, straw, or a hair sieve.

Fermenting Sweet Cider into Hard Cider

Now, up to this point the art of cider making seems clear sailing. The methods of extracting the juice varied over the centuries, but only in tactic, not principle.

When it came to "working" or fermentation—that is, letting

nature take its course so the *sweet* cider could become alcoholic *hard* cider—there was much argument.

The simplest way was to take the sweet cider as it issued from the press into the catching tub, pour it at once into clean wooden barrels or casks, and then carefully regulate the vent. If the vent (the hole or bunghole in the barrel) was too small, fermentation from the natural yeasts in the air would burst open the barrel and hell would break loose in a man's cellar (the barreled stuff had to be stored in a cool place). Painstaking care was exercised so the fermentation would be a long, slow affair. The slower the "working," the better the cider.

From this natural, unhurried, unprocessed method came drinkable natural *hard* cider. But some were dissatisfied with nature's ways and wanted something more potent. They added yeast to the fermentation and they added sugar to the final barrels of stored cider. Some even added apple brandy. Others considered raisins, spices, saltpeter, and alum to be good ingredients for regulating the process and producing better flavor.

The better cider makers, with big presses and the capacity to make cider in vast quantities for resale, eventually abandoned the use of straw to build the cheese and employed haircloth, which could be kept clean and used over and over. They also strained the sweet juice as it ran from the press through a hair sieve into clean open wooden tubs or vats big enough to hold all the juice extracted in one day.

Leaving the liquid to ferment in these open tubs or vats would bring some fine pomace in the solution to the surface and white bubbles would appear. To make sure the sediment (or remaining pomace which had settled to the bottom and was called "lees") did not come with the cider when it was drawn off, a wood faucet or petcock was inserted into the bunghole three inches from the bottom of the container. Through this the clear cider was drawn, leaving the lees on the bottom. Then the cider drawn from the old barrel was poured into clean casks. As soon as bubbles appeared at the top bunghole of the new casks, it was drawn off again (a process called "racking") and poured into clean casks once more.

When the fermentation finally ceased after several rackings, the cider was once again poured into clean barrels and bunged up tight. Now it was left to stand in a cool place until the new product, *hard* cider, acquired the "proper flavor."

What constituted proper flavor was a matter of many judgments. The good cider maker gained enviable repute in his community when the proper flavor was achieved and was agreed upon by his neighbors. The decision as to how many rackings cider needed was a matter of experience and of taste. When the cider maker saw that the liquid was fairly clear and bright and had a winy taste and when he could no longer hear a hissing noise or discover enough pressure to blow out a candle flame held to the bunghole, he would halt the fermentation.

The cider maker knew that the best cider of the proper flavor resulted from keeping the bunged-up barrels in a cellar where the temperature did not exceed 50° F. and never fell too far below 40° F. He knew, too, that if the cider was left in too warm a place and not bunged, but exposed to the air, fermentation got out of hand and the cider became harsh and rough and not drinkable by connoisseurs. If it was kept at a low temperature, all the sugar in the cider was sure to be turned into alcohol, which remained in the solution—a desirable achievement.

The careful cider maker did not rest content with the process as described thus far. When the "proper flavor" had been achieved, he drew off the cider and put it into clean barrels that were sulphured by burning a clean rag dipped in sulphur in the bunghole or by rinsing the inside of the barrel with a solution of bisulphite of calcium (a gallon of water and a fourth of a pound of the sulphite).

All manner of interesting and curious ideas were applied in those days to "manage" cider before it was deemed fit to drink. One recipe called for a gallon of cognac, a pound of alum, half an ounce of cochineal (we wonder if this turned the cider red), and two pounds of rock candy! The solid ingredients were pounded into powder in a mortar and pestle and allowed to stand in the brandy for two days before being mixed into a barrel of cider. Cider, after half a year of storage, was palatable.

The Story of One Old Cider Maker

Fortunately for posterity and for this book, New England still harbors one old-time cider maker who, at eighty, makes cider the old-fashioned, traditional New England way.

Like all New England eccentric geniuses, this man holds firm and often unpopular opinions about his craft. Nine out of ten existing cider mills still operating in rural regions will take any apples they can get and make a kind of cider of them, but our friend will not allow in his cider mill an apple that has been ruined by toxic chemical sprays.

I know this man well because for many years I have bought old-time natural cider vinegar from him. The vinegar he makes of native unsprayed apples seems twice as strong as the vinegar sold in supermarkets. It has never been hydrogenated, homogenized, or treated with sulphur or any other chemicals to "keep" it. It is truly a natural product.

I refuse categorically to reveal his name or even his general location. This is done not just because I wish to protect him from an army of the curious, who would descend upon him and prevent him from making cider and vinegar. I want, more than that, to protect the natural product he makes. Were his whereabouts generally known, I can only guess what kind of exploitation would ensue. Vast conglomerates that know nothing about cider, vinegar, or even food would vie to buy him out, change his product, destroy its quality, and replace one of the best cider makers I have ever known. I respect his independence. I respect his inimitable product. And I respect, above all, his privacy. There is so little of these things in the world today.

Our friend's cider mill is of historic importance because it is constructed in the same way cider mills were 150 years ago. Built into an embankment on top of which runs a road, the building has one story on top of the hill and two on the bottom. This arrangement makes it easy to drive a truck into the top floor through an open door and unload, by the bushel basket or box, apples ready for cider making.

Built into and right under this top floor is the machine that crushes the apples into pomace. This apparatus has teeth fixed into a revolving cylinder, run now by an electric motor but originally run by steam power. As the apples are emptied into the hopper in the floor, the apparatus turns and the apples are crushed almost as fast as a man can fill the hopper.

For some reason I could never make out (and I was there in July), the storage space on the top floor of this old mill was cool, apparently at a temperature just right for storing apples ready for the hopper. Yet I was told that no refrigeration was used. Because of this freak of nature, the cider mill, run like the early New England farm mills, could and did make cider the year round, or until one season's stock of apples ran out.

The pomace-crushing machine in the floor fed into a wood spout so that the ground-up pomace could run down and empty into the press on the ground floor below. The iron press was about 8 feet high and 12 feet long. The heavy platen on top was attached by a series of gears and pulleys to a motor which lowered the platen and the pressboards.

New York State Historical Association, Cooperstown, N.Y.

"The Cider Mill" by William T. Carlton

At one end of the huge press was a 4-foot-square trolley platform on wheels. Heavy coarse cloths were laid on the floor of this trolley, and on top of the cloths was a square wood frame 5 inches deep. The pomace was poured into this frame. As it piled up inside the frame, it was leveled off even to the top. The frame was then removed and the cloth on four sides folded over and around the thick layer of pomace. On top of this layer were placed the pressboards. The process was repeated until there were eight layers. This entire section, on wheels, was then rolled forward and stopped directly under the huge press, which was ready for action.

This old cider maker prefers Russet apples, mixed with Northern Spy and New England Hubbardston. From each bushel of this mixture he calculates that he presses two to two and a half gallons of cider.

He also swears by charred oak barrels, which he buys from whiskey distillers. He believes that such barrels make the best cider. He figures that natural hard cider with nothing added will become 6% alcohol; adding sugar or honey to the mixture raises the alcohol content to about 12%.

At one time many years ago, this cider mill was owned by a man who operated a large hotel in a large city. Our friend told me the story of how the hotel man would build up hard cider with additives to obtain the top potency and then bottle the brew in champagne bottles with the corks wired down. When the hotel was required to give big parties and serve champagne of no specific brand, the waiters plied the guests two times around with real French champagne. But on the third and subsequent servings, the homemade cider drink, with the same sparkle, the same look, and certainly the same alcoholic content, was purveyed. None of the guests, it was said, knew the difference by that time. But there was a difference. In those days, in a hotel, the best Pol Roger or Mumm's extra-dry champagne from France was billed to the host at $10 a bottle. Doubtless, the country champagne made from cider cost less.

MODERN PRINCIPLES

In the foregoing section I have told of old-fashioned methods of cider making used in this country up to the end of the nineteenth century. I have described them in terms of their historic interest, but the basic reason for setting them forth is to show that, in general, although methods and apparatus have changed, today's principles are quite similar.

It may appear repetitive, therefore, to devote another section to modern principles, since they are similar. However, in all commercial plants today and even in some country cider presses, up-to-date methods and apparatus are so different that an outline will serve as a handy and useful guide to those who have large apple orchards and wish to make large quantities of cider.

We Begin with Apples

Everybody agrees that, though there is much cider carelessly and badly made, good cider today starts with the careful discrimination and selection of apples.

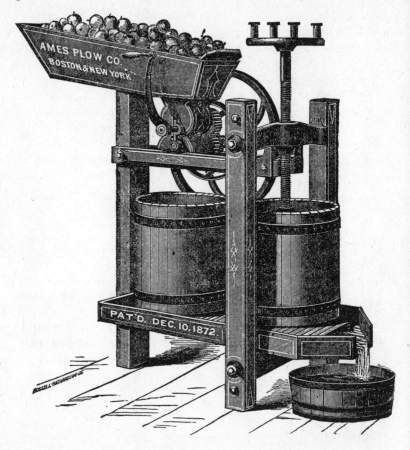

Apples are selected for condition, maturity, and variety.

Good, sound, firm apples ripe enough to eat are the best. Apples that are too green or too far gone lower the quality of the cider. Apples should be picked from the trees by hand or taken off the ground as soon as they fall. Apples that fall to the ground and are allowed to stay there for more than a day acquire an earthy taste which taints the cider. *Sound* apples mean apples that are not bruised, wormy, or have rotten patches. All apples should be carefully washed to remove any foreign matter (dirt). Certainly, sprayed apples should be thoroughly washed, especially around the stems, to get off all vestiges of poisonous chemical spray.

It is preferable to select apples at the peak of their natural maturity, but green fruit that is properly stored in a cool room after harvesting can be kept until maturity.

A note on these points has come from an interview with Walter H. Hildick, Jr., president of Sterling Cider Company, one of New England's oldest commercial producers of cider and cider products.

Mr. Hildick told me: "The primary requirement for the good juice is to start off with good, sound fruit, thoroughly washed and rinsed with clean, unpolluted water, and then promptly pressed, filtered, and bottled in a sanitary manner. New England has long been noted for its fine-flavored apples. More apples are grown in the state of Washington than in any other state, and they are beautiful. But for flavor, New England fruit is superior. We were informed by a leading orchardist years ago that the primary reason for this is that the soil of New England is made up of glacial deposits left here many centuries ago, rich in minerals and trace elements, which make the fruit so healthful and so flavorful. The soil on the West Coast, however, consists largely of volcanic ash and seems to lack something that New England soil has."

Mr. Hildick emphasized that even more important to good cider than the region where apples are grown was the selection of sound *whole* apples. "Mills that make applesauce must peel and core the fruit first. To throw away these peelings would be wasteful, so for many years they were utilized to make cider vinegar. The finished vinegar thus made could be filtered to look attractive and appear as good as vinegar made from the whole, fresh fruit. But much flavor was lost. If these apple peelings and cores are ground and pressed promptly, the result is not too bad, but frequently such apple trimmings are transported from the mill in which they were accumulated to another mill for pressing. After lying around for a while, oxidizing in the air, attracting flies and vermin, the resulting garbage is scarcely fit for human consumption. Often, peeled apples are not even washed first, so that all the dirt and any spray residue adhering to the skins is carried into the juice extracted from them in concentrated form. Today, not only vinegar but also much apple juice is made from such material, yet the Food and Drug Administration has never required any statement on the label that the product is made from anything but good, sound, whole apples. The general public is unaware that it is anything but that."

I cite Mr. Hildick at length to emphasize how important it is, in making good cider today, to exercise painstaking care in the selection and treatment of apples.

Today all authorities agree that one apple variety alone does not make good cider and that a blend results in cider with a finer balance of sweetness, tang, aroma, and body. Two varieties might be sufficient, but three or more are preferable. How to choose the apples is an age-old question. It mostly depends on individual taste. One should know the apples and taste them to develop the proper criterion.

Because the demand these days for good country cider, or any good natural country product, is increasing, the U.S. Department of Agriculture has begun to pay more attention to cider making and has updated its bulletins on the subject. For the convenience of cider makers, it has divided apples into four groups: (1) *Sweet:* varieties grown for eating raw, like Baldwin, Hubbardston, Rome Beauty, Stark, Delicious, Grimes, Cortland. (2) *Mildly acid to slightly tart:* Winesap, Jonathan, Stayman, Northern Spy, York Imperial, Wealthy, Rhode Island Greening, Newton-Pippin. (3) *Aromatic:* Golden Delicious, Winter Banana, Ribston, Transcendent, Martha. (4) *Crab apples:* very astringent, highly acid, and rich in tannin. Tannin has an antiseptic influence on the bacteria which cause bad cider. A little tannin, therefore, acts as an inhibitor of enzymes and makes cider keep longer and better. Only small amounts of crab apples should be used in a blend, however.

It is too bad that one of the favorite apples of old-fashioned cider makers is seldom grown today. I refer to the Russet. Fifty to seventy-five years ago, almost every sizable New England apple orchard grew Russets, because this brown apple packed into its small size a lot of the potent juice that cider makers favored.

Today, if one explores the back country of northern New England and is able to discover what used to be called an "abandoned farm," he will doubtless find an old tree that needs pruning but still has a few Russets clinging desperately to the withered branches.

Despite government nomenclature and the grouping of apples according to sugar, acid, and tannic content, no two cider makers would agree on how to create the proper blend. Yet no one disagreed that apples should be blended. The general rule most cider makers favored was one-third tart, late-fall or winter apples and two-thirds sweet, mid-fall apples. It was accepted that most small apples have a somewhat bitter taste and therefore should be used in a lesser proportion in the blend than larger and sweeter varieties. One maker did not think too much of Delicious apples, which in his experience, if used in too great a proportion in the blend, produced an "insipid" juice. A common and easy practice among small cider makers was always frowned upon by the experts. This was using for cider any apples on hand that could not be eaten or sold for other purposes.

Another expert pomologist condemned certain apples as lacking in flavor, such as Rome Beauty and Ben Davis, but favored the Rhode Island Greening, the Twenty-Ounce, and the Spitzenburg.

These few citations demonstrate the divergent views of both apple experts and cider makers in the selection of apples for a blend. A recent study of New York state apples show a distinct trend: forty years ago, only 10% of all apples raised in New York were processed into apple products such as applesauce, apple slices, syrup, candy, jelly, and apple juice. Today over two-thirds of the New York apple crop is so processed. This would seem on the face of it to indicate that home cider makers are going to have a smaller choice of apples available for cider making. However, studies at the State Experiment Station in Geneva, New York, show that in recent years the growth of country sales outlets for apple cider and the more lively public interest in cider have been recognized by apple growers, and the choice is now actually greater.

Cornell University's Experiment Station published a preliminary study in 1972 on this subject. It appears that bumper apple crops, at least in New York, have provoked a new interest in apple growing, and an expanding market exists for apples for juice and cider.

Making Pomace

Regardless of apple varieties selected for the blend, it is absolutely necessary, as the second step in cider making, to crush, chop, or grind the apples into the pulp called pomace.

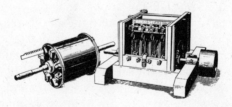

Modern methods utilize power machines: a grater and a hammer mill. The grater (illustrated here) is a simple machine with ¼-inch serrated steel teeth projecting from a cylinder which revolves at high speed. The cylinder is housed in a stout metal cover leaving only about 1/16 of an inch space between the housing plates and the teeth. Such machines are made in all sizes to break up from eight to several hundred bushels of apples per hour. They are, of course, run by electric motors.

The grinding of the fruit into fine pomace is also accomplished by the hammer mill (illustrated), now used by most modern commercial makers. This machine has a round shaft with steel bars like hammers that revolve at high speed inside a heavy housing. A perforated screen in mesh sizes from ⅜ inch to ¾ inch reduces the apple mixture to the right consistency.

There are two types of cider presses today. One is the mechanical device that presses with heavy threaded screws. The other type operates with a hydraulic ram which forces down the top platen and the several pressboards to exert pressure on the pomace placed in the machine. These modern cider presses are in principle like the old-time machines, and the manner of building up the layers to make the "cheese" with pressboards and folded-over press cloths is still somewhat the same. These new presses range in size from a 17-inch to a 52-inch square for holding the pomace. With the smallest, you can press from two hundred to three hundred gallons of cider a day if you work ten hours. The average yield is about eight gallons of cider from a hundred pounds of apples.

Keeping Sweet Cider

You don't have to keep it, you can drink it at once. You can, in polite society, pour the fresh sweet cider out of a jug into glasses or beer mugs. Or you can, as country folk do, learn to balance a jug on one shoulder and, holding the handle with two fingers, drink out of the spout. This is the sweet cider of tradition.

A slightly more refined product can be produced by taking the cider as it has been strained into a vat or tub and arranging for it to "settle" for a spell. It used to be done, as we have described, by running it into barrels and racking. Today it is poured into a sanitary stainless-steel or glass tank and kept at a constant temperature of 40° F. so that some of the precipitated pomace still in solution will settle to the bottom, giving a clearer but still sweet cider. The control of the temperature prevents fermentation for the two or three days required for settling. The juice can then be drawn off by siphoning, or by opening a petcock three or four inches from the tank bottom where the sediment has collected. In commercial and more elaborate operations, sediment is removed by sophisticated methods such as heat treatment, centrifuging, and filtration with certain preparations of enzyme clarification.

There are many ways to "preserve" cider. By this we mean, keep it sweet and safe from fermenting into alcohol.

Refrigeration is the easiest. Immediately after the sweet juice comes from the refrigerated settling vat just described, it can be kept sweet and good for a week or two, without danger of its turning into alcohol if placed at a temperature of no more than 35° and not less than 32°.

Freezing is considered the best. Frozen sweet cider will remain in its natural state for a year. Make sure you fill the glass or plastic containers only to 90% of capacity, to allow for expansion when frozen.

Pasteurization will keep cider sweet almost indefinitely. It is sometimes known as "flash pasteurization," because it is accomplished by heating the liquid to 170° F. for only ten minutes.

Heating longer will create a cooked flavor which is undesirable for cider you wish to taste sweet and fresh. This process must be controlled by a metal-stem thermometer: glass will break. The U.S. Department of Agriculture recommends a homemade pasteurizer that can be put together by anyone. Plans are available from the Eastern Utilization Research and Development Division, Agriculture Research Service, U.S. Department of Agriculture, 600 East Mermaid Lane, Philadelphia, Pa. 19118.

Ultraviolet irradiation is another process commercially employed to keep sweet cider sweet. Ultraviolet light destroys most of the microorganisms that are bound to turn sweet cider into something else.

Last, there are *chemical agents* that will preserve cider. One is potassium sorbate, but it is certainly not recommended; there are too many hazards.

The reason freshly made cider will not stay that way without treatment is that apple skins are covered with all kinds of invisible but very active bacteria and yeast strains, all of which act without invitation. Most English writers on the subject recommend using Campden tablets, sold by wine-making suppliers, from whom full directions can be obtained.* A Campden tablet dissolved in a bit of warm water and added to each gallon of sweet cider will cut down or destroy the work of the yeast and bacteria.

You may wish to keep sweet cider sweet so it won't turn into hard cider. If you're going to drink it soon, you certainly don't want it to turn into vinegar. And the active organisms mentioned may do that little trick, unless you slow them down.

The best containers for sweet cider are gallon and half-gallon glass or plastic jugs. Sterilization is recommended for all containers. Screw tops with rubber gaskets instead of cardboard linings will give you a tight seal on the jugs. Although cider can be and has been canned, the process is not for the amateur.

Regardless of what you are going to do with it, the quality and life of cider in all its stages depends upon the cleanliness of the containers and of every single utensil or machine with which cider

* See Appendix.

comes in contact. Dirty and even slightly unsanitary equipment not only will produce nasty cider, but the accentuated growth of microorganisms will cause incorrect fermentation and strange and unnatural flavors. The need to wash, scrub, clean, and rinse cannot be too strongly emphasized. This includes not just the equipment and the press cloths but the walls and ceiling of the place where the cider is being made. Cider is almost as volatile as milk. Take a note from modern dairies where milk for human consumption is processed. If you keep your place and your cider equipment as clean as milkmen do theirs, you'll have the best cider. However, never never use soap or detergent to clean your equipment. Use hot water only.

A word of caution before we leave the subject of keeping cider as sweet as you can. Professor LaBelle reinforces this caution by once again dwelling on the difference between *cider* and *apple juice*. Processing of sweet cider such as heating or the addition of ascorbic acid to prolong shelf life produces "apple juice" and *not* apple cider! Fresh cider will stay sweet if it is flash-pasteurized, sealed into containers while it is still hot (screw-topped jugs work well), and the jars kept tightly closed. But even this, Dr. LaBelle warns, may produce a slightly *different* flavor from that of the virginal sweet cider before treated. If one wants sweet cider, he favors, as do I, keeping it refrigerated. However, the most sensible course is to drink it before any change can happen. Certainly in these days when chemical or other additives are anathema to many, the man wanting natural sweet cider is warned to eschew tampering with nature.

After all is said and done, sweet natural cider, even after most of the sediment is removed from the liquid, will be somewhat opaque in its natural state. There is nothing wrong with this except looks. As with orange juice, if you want to retain the natural look, you can shake well before using.

The customer for sweet cider has an easy time compared to the producer, who must choose between the possibility of ruining the natural taste of sweet cider by treatment to insure a little longer shelf life and the possibility of losing his product altogether by having it turn sour before he sells it.

Fermentation

Fermentation is one of nature's most controversial activities. It was not invented by man. It happens spontaneously, whether in milk, wine, beer, maple sap, or cider.

The question in cider making is, how do you want it? And what do you want to produce with it?

You can produce plain hard cider, sparkling cider, champagne cider, or dry cider, to mention only a few names for cider with alcoholic content. And there are as many methods, some of which are complex, as there are products.

First, there is a very easy method. Draw off some sweet cider and pour about three and a half quarts into a gallon glass jug, leaving room at the top for fermentation action. If you don't do anything more than keep the jug at room temperature, the cider will start "working" and you will come up with hard cider. It may be sour and it can taste terrible. To improve it you can, before pouring the cider into the jug, add about a fourth teaspoonful of champagne or wine yeast. Just lay the cap on loosely and keep the jug in a cool room. The yeast starts working in a day or so, and then you can drink the cider. This is the lazy man's way. I think there are better ways.

One better way is to watch and control the natural fermentation as the old cider makers did. The most important step at this point is to keep the fermenting cider in a cool place, preferably a cellar, where the temperature is 45° to 50° and no more.

When I buy sweet cider and ferment it at home, this is the way I do it. First, I get a clean, sound, waterproof oak barrel. Caution is advised at this point. A new, freshly made oak barrel, never used before, tends to impart a strong, unpleasant taste to cider. This is not good. To get rid of this taste, you can treat the new barrel with a heavy solution of soda ash and lye and then very thoroughly rinse until it's a hundred percent clean. Even then, some trace of astringents and tannins may remain. One better way is to get a barrel that has been used many times for wine so that the bad flavors have been removed. A still better way is to buy a barrel used to age whiskey or brandy; such barrels have very

little if any deteriorative flavors left. If you buy a new barrel, be
sure you keep it full of water long enough to swell the staves, to
prevent leaking. When the barrel is tight and empty, I take it
down to the cellar and fill it up with sweet cider through a top
round hole (the bung) until a small air space is left under the
barrel top. Then I leave the top bung open and let nature take
its course.

But I watch it and make sure the temperature never goes over
50° F. or under 40° F. I want to come up *not* with vinegar, and
not with rough, hard, bitter cider, which results when the
temperature is too high. I want to get what Hemingway drank,
the one the English call *dry* cider. This simply means that every
bit of sugar in the cider is changed into alcohol to form a tasty,
healthy drink, with a modest alcoholic content.

I watch it day and night. Fermentation will, of course, start in
about one day, sometimes less. If it "works" too fast, because of
too much sugar or too high temperature, I must slow it down to
insure the longest possible period of fermentation. This can be
done by dissolving one Campden tablet to a gallon, or by moving
the barrel into a cooler place, say the cool vegetable section of the
cellar. A good cider maker carries a thermometer at all times.
A man who is fermenting a little cider (say, a couple gallon
jugs) can perhaps sell his wife on the idea of throwing out food
so he can place the jugs in her refrigerator.

If the "working" is too slow, that is, when I hear no hissing,
see no little white bubbles, and the liquid appears lifeless, I must
add some sugar to speed the fermentation or to restore it. I do
this the way I cook. I take a "little" white sugar, mix in a bit of
cider saved for this purpose, and pour this liquid in the barrel.
If I want to be scientific and do it the way my wife cooks (which
means measuring everything properly), then I have to use a
hydrometer. This device, as everyone knows, gives a specific
gravity reading, which translated means, it tells how much sugar is
in a liquid. If the hydrometer reads 1.070 (meaning .07 sugar),
the resulting cider will come up to about the normal alcoholic
content.

How long does this take? Like the cook who says you bake

"until done," I leave the "working" alone until the bubbling or hissing of the gas has subsided completely. But I have to be sure there is no wait once it subsides. The minute the process ends, I want to be there to take the next step.

I will have ready another clean, water-tight barrel with a top bunghole to be plugged. Through this hole I siphon the fermented cider* (wine makers' catalogs will tell you what to buy to do this). Sometimes the cider in the new cask will choose, despite the fact that I have now bunged it up tightly, to work a little longer. If it does (and this will be of short duration), I let it. But I make sure the bunghole is tightly stopped up with a plug and sealed with wax. Unless I have grossly miscalculated and the cider ferments too much and blows out the bung, I am safe in keeping the barrel in the cellar for present and future drinking. The fact is that as soon as this point is reached, the hard cider is ready to drink. Some makers prefer to keep it bunged up tight for months, but after six months it probably won't get any better.

Bottling and Drinking

How may we drink it? We may follow the ways used by our grandfathers. About 3 inches above the bottom of the barrel, which is now seated on a platform of planks off the cellar floor, should be a wood petcock. Open it and draw off a pitcher of cold, hard cider and take it upstairs. The cider tastes natural, the acid in it quenches thirst, and the small alcohol content promotes conviviality. It is wholesome, highly flavored, and one's very own.

I must confess, however, that I was never satisfied with drinking cider this way. I want my cider bottled. By bottling, one can get something that comes pretty close in looks and feeling, if not in actual taste, to French champagne. However, I wish to go on record as stating that I do not and never will drink cider or any other liquid directly from the bottle. I like a bottle for the pleasure of pouring the sparkling cider into a thin, lead-crystal

* See illustration on page 63.

wineglass. One of the most outlandish, and to me shocking, habits of the times we live in is that of swilling down drinks from uplifted bottles. No civilized person guzzles from a bottle if a glass or mug is available. For American advertisers to condone and actually promote such a habit is a good comment on these times when manners have been abandoned and social customs of gentlemen and ladies decried.

Bottled hard cider reaches ultimate perfection in about two years. Unless the cork rots, you can keep it for twenty years.

There are many ways to bottle cider. Let us go back to the point where you put the new fresh sweet cider into the first barrel. Dissolve about four quarts of strained honey in warm water and add this to a 36-gallon barrel. Watch fermentation as before. When the "working" is over and you bottle the liquid, you will eventually have sparkling cider or champagne cider. Before siphoning off the cider from the barrel *after* fermentation, leave the bung out and let the brew stand that way for about twelve hours to allow the fermentation gas to escape. This saves broken bottles—and loss of liquid. After drawing off the cider and filling each bottle from the pitcher, let the cork stay loose in each bottle for twenty-four hours. Then and only then may the corks be forced in with a wood cork plunger and wired down, as in champagne.*

I have made it a practice *not* to use the honey recipe. Instead, I follow what seems to me a surer method, more accurately controlled. After drawing the fermented hard cider from the barrel off into a pitcher (*without* honey in the mixture), I fill each bottle to about one inch from the cork. But first, before filling it, I place a tiny bit of white sugar in the bottom of each bottle. The

* See Appendix.

proper amount of sugar for this purpose is about two ounces per gallon of cider. If you wish to measure and be accurate, you can figure how much to put into each bottle. In a quart bottle you would add no more than a half teaspoonful. This is enough to start secondary fermentation in the bottle and not enough to blow out the cork. When this last fermentation takes place in the bottle (it could be two or three weeks, but you had better wait several months), you will have a delicious sparkling champagne cider fit to drink at any man's table.

A few warnings. Obtain heavy glass bottles that won't break. Use long wet wine corks and plunge them in with a wood corker*

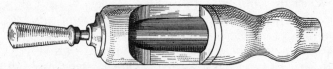

as far as they will go, and then wire them firmly down to the neck of the bottle. Lay the bottles on their sides in a cool dark place to keep the corks moist. If you wish to take a chance and use beer bottles with metal caps forced on with a capping machine, let them stand in the cellar upside down for a while; you may lose a few and you may win a few. If you use empty wine bottles from American vintners, most of these now have a screw-on metal cap, and this, tightened and covered with wax, will usually do to hold in the cider.

Some cider makers are not content with using sugar or honey to bring about a neat sparkling drink. They experiment by adding, before fermentation, all manner of things such as wine spirit, maple sugar, molasses, pure alcohol, cognac, bourbon whiskey, and God knows what else, to perk up the beverage. I suspect that most such diabolic concoctions perk it up right away from cider into something else entirely. This something else may have a high alcoholic content and may give the drinker a big kick, but it is not the natural cider of American tradition.

Neither are certain concoctions recently featured in numerous television promotions. In the last couple of years, several drinks

* *For corker,* see Appendix.

have been placed on the market that, one would think by reading
the statements made by their manufacturers (and the word *manu-
facturer* is apt), are equal to, if not better than, rare French wines
or even the best natural wines that California produces. These
new beverages are manufactured from various fruit juices, some
natural like apple juice and some, one suspects, synthetic, plus a
large amount of grain alcohol. Such mixtures are about as "natural" as the bathtub gin that desperate drinkers once mixed with
ginger ale and, to their later consternation, drank. I don't say that
these new synthetic concoctions are more dangerous than any
liquid to which grain alcohol is added. But they do not in any
respect merit consideration in a book devoted to natural beverages. The only reason I mention them here is to offset the letters
I know will come to me and my publishers asking why I did not
give a recipe for these new drinks. As a matter of fact, I *have*
given one. To repeat: take any fruit juice you have on hand and
add alcohol.

I am glad to report, however, that all wines produced from apple juice are not synthetic. In fact, there is an encouraging new interest in creating genuine natural wines from apple cider. One of the most scientific and up-to-date plants making a natural apple wine was recently established in Vermont.

To the sweet cider they add sugar to double the original sugar content of the cider. Thus, when fermentation of this liquid was completed and all the sugar changed into alcohol, instead of the expected 6% to 7%, this apple wine assayed 12% alcohol. This, of course, is the average percentage of alcohol in natural still wines.

Throughout the process from sweet cider to the bottled wine, no preservatives or artificial agents of any kind are used. The wine is fermented in stainless-steel tanks with temperature controls. Racking to clear the liquid of lees (pomace) in the solution is accomplished at this plant by transferring the liquid, after secondary fermentation, from one large fiberglass tank to another. No fining agents, to clarify the wine, are employed.

A good example of a modern electric hydraulic cider press, from Day Equipment Company (See appendix)

Modern Commercial Cider Making

Most people, and I confess that I was one until I looked into the facts, visualize the cider maker as a farmer with an old-fashioned cider press in his shed. It is true that country cider is still made this way. The greatest number of presses is in New York state; twenty years ago there were three hundred, and today, about a hundred and fifty. Estimates from the International Apple Institute in Washington, D.C., indicate that as many as a million bushels of apples are annually turned into cider by these country presses. Most of this cider is marketed at roadside stands and in local stores. The decline in the number of presses shows that they are going out of existence. This may be due, in part, to increasing production from larger commercial cider plants.

The extent to which commercial cider and cider products are made today is surprising. There are at least a hundred such enterprises in the United States.* In 1971 these plants used 22 million bushels of apples for apple juice and related products. At the average yield of 3.7 gallons per bushel of apples, this adds up to a lot of juice. The large operations are mostly in California, New York, New England, Michigan, Colorado, and Washington. California has about ten large plants. One of the largest and oldest is Martinelli of Watsonville, California. In 1859 Stephen Martinelli migrated from Switzerland to Santa Cruz County. In 1868 he began producing apple cider. The enterprise is carried on today by the same family and is in the hands of his grandson and namesake, to whom we are indebted for information and several recipes, and whose sparkling cider in champagne bottles has become one of our favorite non-alcoholic beverages. Young Steve Martinelli carries on the quality tradition of his grandfather with pride and produces over one million gallons a year. To the best of my knowledge, he is one of the few U.S. producers making natural sparkling apple juice and sparkling cider with a national distribution. Unlike carbonated soft drinks, his product contains

---

* I wish I had the space to list all these people, as I am sure most readers would be surprised to learn that someone near them is making good cider for sale.

no added sugar and no artificial sweeteners, flavors, colors, or chemical preservatives.

For readers interested in the scientific technology of cider manufacture, the standard textbook is *Fruit and Vegetable Juice* by Donald W. Tressler and Maynard A. Joslyn, published by the Avi Publishing Company of Westport, Connecticut. This book is full of formidable statistics; for instance, Northern Spy apples have an 11.60% sugar content, whereas old-time Russets have only 2.91%. The book also groups juice from the apple into five categories.

(1) *Natural.* Ascorbic acid is used to prevent oxidation of the juice. An American patent issued to R. P. Walrod in 1954 is based on the idea that the only "natural apple juice" is the original juice contained in the apple flesh. The minute this juice is pressed out and exposed to the air, it starts oxidizing and quickly turns into a brown-colored liquid with a different taste. Mr. Walrod's patented method preserves the natural color, aroma, flavor, and appearance of fresh natural juice by introducing ascorbic acid to reverse the process of oxidation. (2) *Crushed.* Apple juice containing a small percentage (3% to 10%) of the fine crushed apple pulp, and often labeled "liquid apple." (3) *Clarified.* The apple juice clarified by a centrifuge to remove most of the apple particles. (4) *Filtered.* A lighter-bodied apple juice from which all the apple pulp has been removed by filtering so the product is clear, brilliant, and the most stable. This is also the most common form of apple juice on the market today. (5) *Unfiltered.* The natural sweet apple juice, oxidized and usually homogenized to create a cloudy, natural-looking product.

The English firm of H. P. Bulmer distributes its cider products in the United States under such trade names as Woodpecker, Strongbow, Pomagne, Cidona, and No. 7. Unlike some American commercial *apple juice* manufacturers, Bulmer produces what we call hard cider and what they call dry cider—cider with an alcoholic content of 6% by volume, either still or carbonated like champagne. Their *Pomagne* has as much as 8% alcohol, and tastes, looks, and is bottled like champagne. Their *Cidona* is a non-alcoholic drink. It is carbonated and has a cider taste like the sparkling sweet cider put out by Martinelli. As this book was written, the HR 9716 Bill is before the U.S. Congress. The bill, if passed, will permit sparkling hard (alcoholic) bottled cider to be taxed the same as still wines are taxed. This presumably will make a difference in sales.

The Hildicks at Sterling

A good example of how commercial cider products are made today is provided by the Sterling Cider Company of Sterling, Massachusetts. Just before this book went to press, we inspected their plant, where Walter Hildick, Jr., and his son, Alan, took us on a complete tour. It was indeed a revelation to learn about the methods that have, by necessity, been developed in recent years for making cider and cider products. These changes have come about not so much for greater efficiency as because in these days of the welfare state the manpower is no longer available.

This old family enterprise at Sterling has followed the New England tradition. Walter Hildick's father started it, and Walter, Jr., and his son, Alan, have developed and improved its operations. The eldest Hildick, in 1912, as far as can be determined, was the first to put on the market a pasteurized and refined apple drink. Because it had undergone these two processes, the beverage was called apple juice, the drink so common today in stores throughout the country. Originally the refining (or clarifying of the cider) was done by old-fashioned isinglass or gelatin. Today enzymes are used. These break down and remove the pectin, permitting the solids to be separated from the juice more readily and simplifying filtration, producing a clear product that stays fresh after pasteurization.

In the Hildicks' plant, thousands of gallons of cider are made and stored daily. There are wooden tanks holding as much as 35,000 gallons each. The Hildicks' products, in addition to apple juice, are blends of apple with other pure juices such as Montmorency cherry, cranberry, and black raspberry. Also produced are cider vinegar, vinegar and honey (a mixture of cider vinegar and light clover honey, highly recommended as a natural tonic and made famous by Dr. D. C. Jarvis in his books *Folk Medicine* and *Arthritis and Folk Medicine*), and a salt-free, oil-free dressing, made of cider vinegar and honey with added herbs and spices, for salads and meats.

One of the outstanding features of the Hildick process is the continuous-flow press which squeezes the juice from five to eight tons of apples per hour. This would turn out, on an average, about a thousand gallons of cider an hour. Such a machine supersedes the old-fashioned hydraulic presses, which exerted 2,500 pounds of pressure per square inch but which are now outmoded.

What impressed us most about the plant was the production-line system, which not only expedites the process but turns out a sanitary product untouched by human hands. From the time the apples are dumped into the big hopper and automatically cleaned, washed, and rinsed, until, passing along the line, they are ground into pulp by a hammer mill, pressed into juice, and fine-screened to remove small particles, the machines are all coordinated. The screened juice is collected in a receiving tank and pumped either to a processing tank for filtration and bottling or to one of the storage tanks, where it is fermented and converted into vinegar.

Also, the production of vinegar is much faster. The old-fashioned vinegar-making technique involved storing the fermented cider in barrels for as long as three years to allow it to acetify into vinegar. At Sterling, without changing the basic natural idea of making vinegar, the time has been shortened to three or four days by the "vinegar generator." Of course, man does not do the trick alone. A host of bacteria act upon hard cider to change it into vinegar by converting the alcohol in the fermented cider to the acetic acid in the vinegar. The "vinegar generator" is a mechanical method of speeding up this conversion by exposing the natural process to greater quantities of oxygen in the air. It may be said that man has found a way to hurry the bacteria.

In all natural vinegar, there is a jelly-like substance, found in the bottom of the barrel or in the generator. This is called the "mother," another word for the gelatinous substance which contains a high concentration of live bacteria. Old vinegar makers took some of this "mother" from one barrel and placed it into another barrel of newly fermented cider to hasten the change to vinegar. When the vinegar has been made and the bacteria have

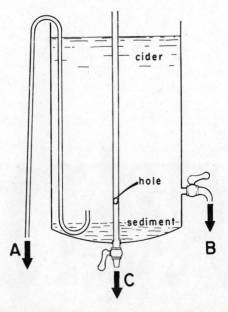

Three methods of drawing cider from the settling tank: (a) *siphoning;* (b) *tapping; and* (c) *draining*

done their work, however, there is no longer any need for the "mother." Its job is over and it may go. This is why modern vinegar makers are amused when they get letters from health-food devotees who ask if they can buy vinegar with the "mother" in it; when there is no longer any use for the "mother," it is thrown out.

3

How to Make Cider
in the Home

*T*o give the impression that a frail housewife can easily squeeze out gallons of cider in her home with small, home-style utensils, and, moreover, that she can do this with little effort and in a short time, would be to give an entirely false and even dangerous impression. Making cider involves work. Using tools and a manual press takes care, patience, and time.

It is a job better for two people than for one. I can do it, and have done it, alone in my kitchen, but it is easier with my wife helping. It also goes faster and is more fun. After all, one of the great and noble functions of womanhood is to stand by and hand things to men to work with.

Let's approach this as we do a cooking recipe. Here are the things you'll need.

Wine press	Apples	Two pails
Wood bowl	Scoop	Sturdy bench
Steel chopper	Slaw slicer	Glass jars
Dish-washing brush	Cheesecloth	

First, wash everything, and I mean everything: the press, bowl, all the tools, jars, pails, and, of course, the apples.

The method of washing apples depends on how much cider you plan to make. If you are going to use only a bushel or two of apples, you can wash each apple in the kitchen sink with a brush to get off dirt, as we do in our house. Take special care to brush off the chemical sprays around the stems. If you are going to make several bushels of apples into cider, the easy way is to dump them on a big cloth on the ground and wash them under full pressure with a stream of water from a hose.

Making Apples into Pomace

Let's face the fact that the finer the pomace, the more cider will be quickly pressed out of the apples with less pressing.

There are several ways to make pomace at home. One way is to use a slaw cutter. This wooden tool is perhaps the oldest kitchen

utensil in existence today. It is still used in Germany to make sauerkraut and also used by American housewives quickly to turn out thin-sliced potatoes, carrots, cabbages (for coleslaw), and other hard fruits and vegetables. If you place the wooden slaw cutter over the bowl and draw apples over it, thin slices of apple will drop into the bowl, where they are ready for chopping. Warning: watch this cutter, and don't wear down the apple to the point where you cut your fingers. Slice the apple along one side, then turn it up and do the other side. The last small piece can be thrown into the bowl for chopping.

You can, of course, do without a slaw slicer. Cut each apple with a knife into small pieces and chop these up in the wooden bowl. This takes longer.

There are also other, hard ways of making pomace, in case you live far from civilization. I know of one couple who dumped apples into a big tub and used a heavy, five-foot-long log to crush the apples into pomace by pounding them with the end of the log, much as a housewife uses an old-fashioned wooden potato masher.

Some cider makers like to let the pomace stand for a day so it will oxidize and turn brown. This is supposed to produce a better-flavored cider. If you haven't the time, however, you can start pressing the pomace almost as fast as your partner can chop it up in the wooden bowl.

Pressing the Pomace

Pressing the juice from the pomace sounds easy, and if you use some methods, it is. It can be done as simply as old-fashioned housewives years ago used to wring the water out of clothes before hand ringers or electric clothes dryers were invented. After the pomace is enclosed in a long, tube-shaped bag of coarse porous sacking, two reasonably strong adults can twist both ends over a vat or tub and press out *some* juice. I do not recommend it but only cite it for the record.

The last time I was in England, I heard about a method of making cider without even having to press the pomace at all! I have neither seen this done nor can I vouch for it. But I was told that after you create the pomace you place it into an open tub and allow nature to take its course. In short, the pulp itself ferments. This natural process may be hastened by adding some sweet syrup; over there they would probably use Golden Syrup, and over here we would use corn or maple syrup. Heaven knows what alcoholic content results. Suffice it to say that after a week or two of natural fermentation some juice actually can be strained out of the pomace and you have a little easy cider without a cider press. The easy way is not always the best way. On the other hand, if I were stranded on the proverbial desert island and had some apples, this method would be better than nothing.

The wooden wine press illustrated here is of the smallest size and just right for home use. The hardwood slats that form the round cage to hold the pomace are 11 inches deep and about 7½ inches in diameter inside. This will hold about a pailful or two gallons of pomace. I set the press on a low, sturdy wooden stand about 18 inches from the floor, because this makes it easier for me to turn the steel rod on top of the screw than if the press were higher.

Inside the cage of the press we place a clean cloth to form a bag, with the edges long enough to fold back over the top of the cage. Good cotton sheeting will do.

Using a wooden scoop or a saucer, you can soon fill the inside area. As you scoop in each measure of pomace, press it down a

little with your hand. Be sure to have a pail on the floor under the spout, as a little juice will start to trickle out at this point. Don't forget to tie several layers of cheesecloth over the top of the pail, so the cider can strain through it as it runs from the press.

When it is full of pomace, fold the cloth over the top and then place the round wooden platen (which has a metal hole for the end of the screw) on top of the cloth and start turning the rod. Screw the platen down slowly; at once cider will begin to run into the groove around the bottom of the press and into the pail below. Pressing should not be done all at once. If you wish to be frugal and obtain the last remaining drop of cider from your pomace, you can expect this process to take as long as a day. Once I started my last batch on Sunday morning, and every half hour during the day I got more juice by pressing the platen down a few more turns. (This process can be accomplished by one man alone, but it's better to have someone else alongside to hold the press so you can use both hands to turn the rod.) After attacking the pomace with more pressure at least ten times that afternoon, I had to leave it until the next morning. I was then able to give the press a dozen more turns and get a pint more of cider. This would have been lost had I been in too great a rush. So, if you can, I recommend that you use the better part of a day to do the pressing. If you want the last drop, let the press stand overnight and go at it again the next morning.

Now the new fresh sweet cider is ready to drink or to keep for converting into hard (dry) cider by fermentation as described in detail on pages 34ff. and 51ff.

The home method is for modest souls who want to use a bushel or two of apples. At most orchards you can buy "utility apples," which means apples orchardists cannot sell as first-grade eating apples. The utility grade will be odd sizes, bruised here and there, but they should not be rotten or wormy. In Vermont at the orchards we can buy, in the fall, such apples for cider at $2 or $2.50 a bushel if we provide our own bags or containers. The orchard people won't give you a free box or basket at that price.

I would like to point out that the home method is fun, especially for children. My three-year-old grandson watched, with keen interest and little patience, the making of the first batch of cider last fall. He wanted to drink it as fast as it issued forth!

The home method is also perfect for folks who have an apple tree and hate to see the apples go to waste.

If, however, a man owns an apple orchard and intends to make many gallons of cider, I certainly recommend that he buy a power machine for crushing the pomace and a power press for squeezing out the juice.*

* See Appendix.

4

Recipes for Cider
in Beverages and in Cooking

When one delves into the hundreds of cookbooks revealing America's domestic cuisine of the nineteenth century, and even more interesting, the folklore of rural America during that period, one is surprised to learn that cider instead of wine was often used as a seasoning in cooking. It is natural that this should be so; wine was an exotic and alien substance to rural folk, but cider was common, readily available, and cheap.

Most housewives, however, discovered for themselves, without the aid of cookbooks, how to cook with cider. Although New England rural women usually received a wedding present of a cookbook such as *Fanny Farmer's,* most of them had learned cooking at home from their mothers. And like their mothers and grandmothers they kept scrapbooks in which they wrote favorite recipes they had tried or been told about. It is a telling comment that old-fashioned rural women had few cookbooks but cooked far more than their contemporary descendants who, these days, collect shelves of cookbooks but have little time for cooking. In early times, women had not succumbed to the magic lures of golf, club life, social service, and other extracurricular activities, nor had they been obliged to act as chauffeurs for their children. They had time to cook at home. And this was how they discovered two basic facts about cooking with cider. First, they learned that it actually was a seasoning and not only improved the flavor of foods but enhanced the natural flavors of many dishes put on the family table. These women either knew or sensed the fact that the alcohol boils away. The use of cider in cooking was a sound temperance practice, therefore, because all that was left was the taste and not the alcohol. Second, these cooks discovered that hard cider in cooking acted as a food tenderizer. This became apparent in using cider for sauces and for basting roasts and was demonstrated chiefly in creating marinades. Marinating meat with cider in place of wine before cooking gave the meat a piquant flavor and most certainly helped make it more tender.

There are not too many concoctions created in the kitchen that are not improved by wine or cider. This includes all kinds of foods, from soups to desserts with, of course, some exceptions. For example, you can't use cider in soups made with milk. For all other soups the general rule is: use a half cup of cider to a quart of soup.

In our kitchen we have found that a good, general rule for cooking with cider is this. Use sweet cider in recipes calling for *Sauterne* wines. In those that require *Chablis,* or other dry French or Rhine wines, use hard cider, or a dry cider containing alcohol.

A word of caution. Don't expect to get good results by using cider in place of fortified wines (sherry and port) or of heavy sweet wines such as Tokay, Muscatel, or Marsala. Cider in any form will *not* do as a substitute for red Burgundies or other red wines. Think of cider as you would *white* wines and you'll be safe, and come up with some delicious dishes in the American fashion.

It cannot be overemphasized that the use of cider in cooking is only for the taste or flavor of the cider, as is the use of wines. Therefore, a great deal of experimenting by a cook in learning the taste of cider and how it comes through in the cooking process may be needed to determine how he or she likes it and can use it.

In Normandy, the major cider-producing region of France, many native recipes for cooking call for "white wine *or* cider." This is particularly true in sauces such as *Sauce Normande* for fish and meat, *Sauce Rouennaise* for wild duck, or in that famous dish *Tripes à la mode de Caen*. In these cases a dry cider is called for; that is, a cider that has all its sugar changed into alcohol.

It must be kept in mind that if you use *sweet* cider in cooking, you should be prepared to have it caramelize and darken food.

This book on American cider does not advocate the use of cider *instead* of wine. The captivating flavors of good wines, so long a part of the traditional and noble cuisine of France, are not to be abandoned. Our intent is, rather, to suggest to the imaginative American cook that the use of cider in cooking gives her *another* flavor to work with and opens many delightful opportunities for her to exercise her inventive genius.

A Note on Old-Time Recipes

It should be explained, first of all, that measurements of seventy-five years ago or more were somewhat different from those of today. In the old days, for example, cooks used whole ginger-root, but because today's commercial *powdered* ginger is much stronger, you must use less of it. Another example: one whole nutmeg, which looks so small, when grated on a tin grater is the equivalent of three tablespoons of today's prepared powdered nutmeg. There is also much confusion about the word "cup." Cups were different in size then; a measuring "cup" in the old recipes was about six ounces, instead of the full eight ounces of modern measurements. A "pinch" of salt or herb flavoring was about a fourth of a teaspoon, depending, of course, on the size of your finger and thumb.

Wholegrain meal or flour, once known as "Graham Flour," was named after a famous medical doctor who wrote a book advocating the use of meal or flour stone-ground to preserve 100% of the wheat kernel.* The whole kernel of wheat slowly stone-

ground into flour, with nothing left out, should be purchased directly from places that mill their own grains and sell flour fresh from the stones. If kept on store shelves for any length of time, natural flour turns rancid because it contains the germ of the wheat. A book could be written on the principles of old-fashioned cooking, but the above will suffice as an admonition when you use our old-time recipes for cooking with cider.

* For further detail, see *Cooking with Wholegrains* by Mildred Ellen Orton.

WARNING

I beg of you, gentle reader, before you try these recipes, please be warned that I am not responsible for your results. Cooking requires not only patience and some talent and imagination but above all a knack that comes with time. It is as senseless for a cook to expect a cookbook to guarantee complete, instant, and irrevocable success as it would be for a composer to guarantee that his music could be rendered perfectly, without practice, by one and all.

I am the author of other recipe books. I do not live a week without getting letters and telephone calls from my valued readers asking me for advice on why a certain recipe did not "come out well" or what would happen if they changed my directions or what would I think of new ideas they have come up with. This is all very pleasant, but I have been advised by my attorneys that I cannot establish an advisory service, or I should be responsible for the results.

For this reason, I must assure the readers of this volume that I cannot undertake to discuss or debate the subject of cooking with cider. I can only say, in self-defense, that all I know about cider is in this book. It is not perfect, or complete, and there is no claim made that it is the ultimate word. What is? Cider is a fascinating but complex subject. And as I said earlier in this book, cider is capable of perfection, but man, in spite of William Godkin's thesis, is not and never will be.

CIDER IN BEVERAGES

Early American cookbooks contained, in addition to instructions for making cider, many ways of using cider to make drinks that in themselves were not cider. A few of these are listed here in the interest of history and also to provide suggestions for experimentation today.

Virginia Night Cap (1745)

Mix up about 25 whole cloves in mortar and pestle until fine powder, and into this crush 4 teaspoons sugar. Add this to a blend of a pint of hard cider and 6 oz. cognac, and heat, so it can be taken before bedtime.

General Lee's Posset (1776)

This Lee is not the Confederate general but the other one (Light Horse Harry), who fought in the American Revolution. He took a quart of heavy cream and with this mixed a pint of sweet cider. Then the yolks of 10 eggs were beaten smooth and the whites of 4 eggs the same and this was mixed with the cream-cider liquid. Then one cup Madeira wine and some grated nutmeg were added to the mixture, which was then set over low heat and simmered until the mixture became thick. But it was removed before it got hot enough to boil. Can be served hot or cold.

Stonewall (1780)

For hands while haying, or as a cool summer drink at other times, take whatever quantity of hard cider you will need and into it mix black Jamaica rum, 1 part rum to 2 parts cider. Jug and take out to the fields.

Constitution Flip (1789)

Into 1 pint hard cider dissolve 2 oz. crushed rock candy in which have been crushed a 1-inch-long stick of cinnamon and 2 whole cloves. Now beat one egg as much as you can and add this to the liquid. Stir all. Place in big earthen mug. Plunge a red-hot poker, which you have heated in the fireplace, into the mug. Then drink the mixture.

Mulled Cider (1790)

Place in a heavy cooking dish 1½ quarts hard cider into which are mixed ⅓ cup sugar, ½ teaspoon allspice, and 2 sticks of cinnamon. Add to this ½ cup rum. Heat but do not boil. Strain and serve hot in mugs.

Republic Cider Punch (1791)

½ NUTMEG GRATED	1 CUP GOOD APPLE BRANDY
1 SLICE DARK BREAD TOAST	1½ CUPS SHERRY
6 TEASPOONS BROWN SUGAR	1 QUART SWEET OR HARD CIDER
3 LEMON SLICES	JUICE OF 1 LEMON
CRACKED ICE	1 QUART CHARGED WATER

Grate nutmeg onto the slice of toast placed at the bottom of a punch bowl. Then lay the sugar and lemon slices on the bread. Distribute enough ice around the edges of the toast to cover bottom of the bowl. Now add the brandy, sherry, cider, lemon juice, and the charged water last of all.

Connecticut Syllabub (1796)

The first cookbook published in New England, which was written by an American from Hartford, Miss Amelia Simonds, gives this recipe: "Sweeten a quart of cyder with refined sugar, grate nutmeg into it, then milk your cow into your liquor."

Smooth Syllabub (1800)

Take about 4 oz. brandy and mix into 1 pint hard dry cider. Add to this the juice and scraped rind of 1 lemon, and ¼ lb. sugar. Place in pantry overnight. Then beat 2 cups heavy cream with 2 egg whites previously beaten, and add to the liquid. It is ready.

Artillery Punch (1812)

Bring together 1 quart dark rum, 1 quart bourbon whiskey, and 1 gallon hard cider. Mix. Then slice 6 pineapples, 12 oranges, and a quart of strawberries. Add all fruit to the liquid. Let it stand in punch bowl overnight. The mess sergeant can guard it. When ready, add ice and 12 bottles of champagne to the punch bowl and serve.

Spinster's Night Cap (1829)

Take 2 quarts cold soft water, 9 gallons hard cider, 8 lbs. strained honey, 2 oz. powdered white tartar (or baking soda), and mix with 2 oz. each of cinnamon, cloves, and mace. Add about 2 quarts dark Jamaica rum. Let it all ferment and bung in cask or bottle. Take sparingly.

Red Wine of Cider (1839)

Mix together and put in barrel 16 gallons cider, 3 gallons cold water, 10 lbs. strained honey. Let it all ferment. Now introduce 1 gallon New England rum, 4 lbs. sugar, 4 lbs. beetroot, 6 oz. powdered red tartar, 3 handfuls each of sweet marjoram and sweetbriar, and mix into the first liquid.

Sleeper's Cider (1840)

Combine in a saucepan 1 quart hard cider, 1 teaspoon allspice, 1 teaspoon whole cloves, 2 cinnamon sticks, and simmer under cover for 20 minutes. Strain out the spices and serve hot, each serving with a slice of lemon.

Apple Wine (1860)

To each gallon of cider as it comes sweet from the press add 2 lbs. sugar. Boil it as long as any scum rises, then strain it through a sieve and let it cool. Add some sourdough yeast and mix well. Let it "work" in a tub for two to three weeks, then skim off the head. Draw it off and pour into sealed barrel. Keep one year, then rack it off into another clean barrel and add 2 oz. isinglass to the barrel. Then add ½ pint spirits of wine to every 8 gallons of the liquid. This will become about 12% strong.

Champagne Cider (1861)

This is an old recipe for a great quantity of this famous drink. Pour 18 gallons hard cider into a barrel. A clean but charred whiskey barrel is preferable. Add 3 pints rectified spirits and 5 pints sugar syrup such as maple or sorghum. Let stand to work, and in three weeks clear with 1 pint skimmed milk, 1 gill orange-flower water, 3 drops neroli. Then bottle in stout bottles, tie down cork, and lay on sides.

Nervous-Headache Medicine (1867)

Steep together 1 quart hard cider, 3 tablespoons white mustard seed, 3 tablespoons burdock seed, and 1 horse-radish root. Keep it all in a tightly corked bottle. Take a wineglass two or three times a day.

Cider Wine (1869)

After new sweet cider has fermented as far as it will, add to each gallon from 1/2 to 2 lbs. white sugar and then allow the liquid to ferment again. When it has done so, extract 1 quart and to this stir in, for each gallon in the total batch, 1/4 oz. *sulphite of lime* (not sulphate). Add all this to the batch that is fermenting. First stir it, and then let the liquid settle. After several days, the resulting cider will be clear. Draw it off by siphon. Bottle and cork.

Lovers' Balm (1872)

Mix 2 tablespoons white sugar into the juice of 1 lemon and the sliced rind of the same, pounded. Let the sugar dissolve in this. Now put this into an earthenware jug and pour in 1/3 cup French brandy, 1/4 cup Curaçao, and 1 quart hard cider. Shake well to mix. Place the jug in a very cold place. When cold enough, pour into a glass until the glass is about half full. Add sparkling water from siphon until the drink fizzes to the brim.

Wives' Nog (1880)

1 PINT HARD CIDER	1/2 TEASPOON GRATED NUTMEG
2 OZ. SHERRY	1/2 ORANGE SLICED
1 OZ. BRANDY	PEEL FROM 1 LEMON
1 OZ. CURAÇAO	1 SLICE CUCUMBER
1 TEASPOON MAPLE SUGAR	

Mix the liquids well, add sugar, nutmeg, and stir in the orange and lemon, topping off with the cucumber.

Cider Smash (1888)

3 SLICES LEMON	SHAVED ICE
SEVERAL SQUARES PINEAPPLE	2 OZ. BRANDY
1 TABLESPOON CONFECTIONERS' SUGAR	CIDER

Drop fruit slices into a tall glass, add the sugar. Fill 3/4 full with shaved ice. Then add brandy, and now cider to fill.

Barley Cider (1890)

Into 26 gallons of sweet cider mix 10 lbs. maple or brown sugar, 4 lbs. raisins, and 4 quarts pearl barley. Add ½ cup oil (probably olive oil). Put the whole into barrel for fermentation, and when that is done hold it, if you can, in a bunged-up cask to age a bit.

Night Cap (1890)

9 EGGS, SEPARATED
4 TABLESPOONS POWDERED
    SUGAR

2 QUARTS HARD CIDER
FRESH GRATED NUTMEG
ALLSPICE

Beat egg whites and then beat yolks with the sugar. Pour cider into an iron skillet and place on stove. Mix whites and yolks in bowl and beat together thoroughly. When cider begins to boil, slowly pour the hot cider into the egg mixture and grate nutmeg and some allspice into the same. Stir and drink. Important: pour cider into eggs; if you pour eggs into cider, they will curdle.

Tisane of Cider (1896)

Tisane usually was heavily laden with herbs. Here is a tisane made with sweet cider, or hard if you prefer.

3 STICKS CINNAMON
7 PINCHES ALLSPICE
2 QUARTS CIDER

1 CUP MAPLE SUGAR
2 WHOLE CLOVES

Mix everything together and boil. Then let the stuff simmer for about 20 minutes. Cool and age it for a day or two and then heat and serve hot on a cold day.

Hot Cider Mug (1897)

Into 3 quarts hard cider mix 1 cup brown or maple sugar, 1 teaspoon each of cloves and allspice, and a little cinnamon. Then let the mixture cook slowly for several minutes until it is blended well. Serve hot in mugs.

Hot Cider Cure (1897)

Into a mortar place 2 teaspoons allspice, 4 short sticks cinnamon, 1 tablespoon whole cloves, 1½ cups brown sugar, and 2 tablespoons grated lemon rind. With pestle mash everything fine and smooth. Mix this into 1 gallon hard cider and heat slowly on back of stove to simmer for about a half hour. Never boil or bubble. Then strain it through a fine sieve and serve. With a nutmeg tin, grate some nutmeg into each glass. Stir with a stick of cinnamon. If this cools off, heat it again.

Vermont Mulled Cider (1908)

2 QUARTS SWEET CIDER	1 TEASPOON GRATED CLOVES
1 TABLESPOON MAPLE SUGAR	1 TEASPOON ALLSPICE
4 STICKS CINNAMON	1 CUP APPLEJACK

Tie the cloves and allspice into a cheesecloth bag and drop this into the cider, sugar, and cinnamon mixture. Boil for 15 minutes, stirring all the while. Then remove cinnamon sticks and the bag of spices, add 1 cup hot applejack, and serve. This is a hot drink in more ways than one.

Hot Spiced Noggin (1909)

Into a saucepan pour ¾ cup maple sugar and a small pinch of salt. Pound up together 2 sticks cinnamon, 1 tablespoon cloves, and a touch of allspice. Add this mixture to 1 quart warm water and pour all into saucepan and bring to a boil. Then let stand on very low heat until everything is well blended. In another pan mix slices of 1 orange and 1 lemon and 2 quarts cider. Heat but do not boil. Now strain this mixture and combine with first mixture. It goes hot into mugs or cups.

Southern Punch (1914)

4 STICKS CINNAMON	GRATED ORANGE PEEL
2 TEASPOONS WHOLE CLOVES	1/2 CUP LEMON JUICE
5 CUPS CIDER	ICE
4 CUPS GRAPE JUICE	2 QUARTS GINGER ALE
GRATED LEMON PEEL	SOME ORANGE SLICES

In a saucepan mix the spices into half the cider and bring to a boil, then let simmer for a few minutes. Now let cool and strain. Into the other half of the cider, pour the grape juice, the peels, and the lemon juice. Chill very cold. Fill punch bowl partly full of ice and in equal parts pour this mixture and the ginger ale over ice. Lay on the orange slices and serve in glasses.

Locomotive (1917)

Heat 1 quart hard cider until hot but not boiling. Into 3 eggs, well beaten until frothy and light, add the hot cider very carefully, a bit at a time. If it cools during the process, heat again to a point just short of boiling. Stir in some white sugar until dissolved. Serve in warmed earthenware mugs, each having a stick of whole cinnamon.

Soda-Fountain Cider (1920)

This modern idea is to cook 1 1/2 cups sugar in 2 cups water for a few minutes, then pour in 1 quart sweet cider, 1 pint orange juice, and 1/2 cup lemon juice. When it's cool, strain. Place in the freezer until it becomes partly ice, and serve.

Temperance Punch (1930)

Into a pitcher of ice place 1 quart sweet cider, 1 small wine-glassful French brandy, 2 oz. sugar, and 1 sliced lemon. Pour into a tall glass half full. Fizz to top with charged water.

French Cider Cup (1936)

In an earthenware, 2-quart pitcher place lots of ice cubes or cracked ice. To this add 1 pint hard cider. Then add 4 teaspoons confectioners' sugar, 1 oz. French brandy, 1 oz. Curaçao, 6 oz. sparkling water, and stir well. When blended, place some slices of orange and fresh mint leaves on top.

Michigan Eggnog (1939)

Into a cocktail shaker put 1 beaten egg, 1 teaspoon confectioners' sugar, 1/2 cup coffee cream, and shake hard, with cracked or shaved ice. Then pour some into a tall glass or frosted mint-julep tankard and fill glass with sweet cider, adding freshly ground nutmeg to the top.

Quick Cider Punch (1940)

Freeze one tray of ice cubes using sweet cider instead of water. Place 1 ice cube in each highball glass. Fill with cold cider and top off with fresh mint leaves.

Frozen Cider Drink (1960)

Take 2 1/2 cups sweet cider and mix in a cup of fresh orange juice. Add cold applesauce and lemon juice and mix in a blender. Freeze until soft enough to spoon out into glasses for a cold drink.

CIDER IN COOKING

General Uses

BAKED BEANS. When you soak the beans overnight, as you should before baking the next day, soak them in cider instead of water.

CORN-MEAL MUSH. Into 3 cups water and 3 cups cider place ½ teaspoon salt. Boil in saucepan, then transfer to double boiler. Slowly add 1½ cups stone-ground corn meal, stirring all the while to avoid lumps. Then cook for one hour.

RICE. For a nice flavor, try soaking ¾ cup of rice in some cider before cooking.

BEARNAISE SAUCE can be made with cider instead of white wine.

BASTING of roasts is improved by using cider instead of water or wine. With melted butter, some juice from the roasting pan, *and* cider, you will enjoy a new taste in roasted meat or turkey.

TURKEY STUFFING can be seasoned with hard cider instead of whatever liquid you normally use.

BAKED SQUASH can be enhanced by cider—enough cider to cover the bottom of the baking dish.

MINCEMEAT, which needs rum or brandy in the making, also needs hard cider. Combined with raisins, currants, candied orange peel, sliced apples, spices, and chopped beef, this will produce a rich mincemeat indeed.

RED PEPPER RELISH and other relishes or chutney can be made with hard cider in place of vinegar.

PIES. When making apple pie, use cider instead of water to moisten crust mixture.

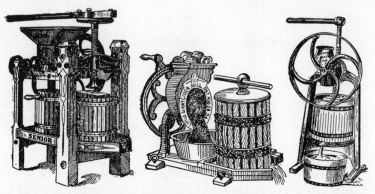

Examples of home cider mills advertised by mail-order houses in 1890

BAKED APPLES will be enhanced if cider instead of water is used in cooking.

SOUPS. One rule to keep in mind is that you can replace the stock called for in soup with the same amount of cider. This works best in pea soup and onion soup.

APPLESAUCE. For making applesauce, sweet cider is always better than water.

GRAVY. In beef gravy a good flavor comes from a mixture of half stock and half hard cider.

FISH. A new taste can be achieved by baking fish, especially mackerel, in hard cider instead of the vinegar and water some recipes call for.

*New England Family Recipes**

Mincemeat

There are dozens of recipes, most cookbooks having several, for making what is called "mock mincemeat." This is mincemeat made without meat. If you make this, use hard cider in all cases in the recipe in place of half the vinegar that recipes call for.

Cider Cakes

There are many interesting cakes made with cider. Though many seem alike, they do vary slightly.

Cider Cake 1

Cider cake is very good baked in small loaves. Mix 1½ lb. flour, ½ lb. sugar, ¼ lb. butter, ½ pint cider, 1 teaspoon pearl-ash. Add spice to taste. Bake till it turns easily in the pans—about 30 minutes.

Cider Cake 2

1 CUP SUGAR	1 TEASPOON NUTMEG
1 CUP BUTTER	1 TEASPOON SALERATUS
2 OR 3 EGGS	1 CUP CIDER
3 CUPS FLOUR	

Mix together sugar and butter and add the eggs. Then add 1 cup flour, nutmeg, and saleratus. Put in 1 cup cider, or pour the cider foaming over it. Then add 2 cups flour. Mix. Bake 45 minutes.

---

* Some of these recipes are from my wife's collection, or her book *Cooking with Wholegrains,* and/or a manuscript collection of old recipes written and used by my maternal grandmother and my mother.

Cider Cake 3

½ TEASPOON NUTMEG	¼ LB. BUTTER
½ TEASPOON SODA	1½ CUPS SUGAR
¼ TEASPOON SALT	2 BEATEN EGGS
3 CUPS FLOUR	½ CUP SWEET CIDER

Combine in a bowl the nutmeg, soda, salt, and flour. Separately, blend butter and sugar, and beat in eggs until smooth. Now stir the second mixture into the first and slowly add the cider, using flour to get the right consistency. Bake in greased pan at about 350° until done (about 1 hour).

Cider Cake 4

1 CUP BUTTER	½ CUP MILK
6 CUPS FLOUR	1 TEASPOON SODA
3 CUPS SUGAR	1 CUP SWEET CIDER
1 NUTMEG, GRATED	

Stir together the butter, 2 cups flour, sugar, nutmeg, and milk, with the soda dissolved in it first. While mixing, stir in the cider and 4 cups flour. Bake until done.

Cider Cake 5

This recipe has no eggs and no milk. It was created by a young lady in 1899.

¾ CUP BUTTER	1 TEASPOON GROUND CLOVES
1½ CUPS MAPLE SUGAR	⅓ CUP SWEET CIDER
1 TEASPOON SODA	4½ CUPS FLOUR
1 TEASPOON GROUND CINNAMON	

Blend the butter and sugar together into a smooth paste. Add the soda and the spices and blend some more. Now blend these ingredients into the cider and combine with the flour until smooth. Bake until done.

Vegetables in Cider

There are several vegetables that take on a new taste if cooked in hard cider. Freshly ground pepper and some salt is added to the cider, and in this liquid you can cook carrots, lima beans, kernel corn, or parsnips.

Game or Fowl with Cider

In an iron skillet, slowly cook the chicken or game bird with butter until brown on all sides. Cover and let simmer on low heat until done. Make a basting of ½ cup sweet cider mixed with a tablespoon of lemon juice. Pour this over the fowl as it cooks, for half an hour.

Cider Sausages

Take a sliced onion and sauté in oil until brown, then remove from skillet. Now roll the sausages in flour and fry until brown. Pour off the fat and add the sautéed onion and then add 1 sliced apple and ½ pint hard cider. Cover pan and let simmer for half an hour.

Filet of Sole in Cider

Melt 2 teaspoons of butter in a baking pan and sift in some fine-ground parsley. Take 6 filets of sole or other fish, salt and pepper them to taste, and place in the pan. Over the filets add a mixture of 3 gobs of butter, some bread crumbs, and more parsley. Salt again and add 1 cup hard cider. Bake at about 350° for 10 minutes.

Veal Chops with Cider

First salt and pepper about 6 veal or lamb chops to taste. Then mix 2 big gobs of butter with ½ cup chopped onion and pour this over the chops in a baking dish. Use a cup hard cider to baste the chops while cooking.

Vermont Mincemeat

4 LBS. BEEF   3 TABLESPOONS SALT
3 LBS. SUET   1 BOX SEEDED RAISINS
12 LBS. APPLES   4 LBS. BOILED PIECES OF BEEF
3 LBS. CHOPPED SUET   1 QUART BARBADOS MOLASSES
6½ LBS. MAPLE OR BROWN   10 TABLESPOONS CINNAMON
    SUGAR   5 TABLESPOONS NUTMEG
2 QUARTS BOILED CIDER   1 TABLESPOON GROUND PEPPER
4 TABLESPOONS CLOVES   1 QUART APPLEJACK

Boil 4 lbs. of beef and 3 lbs. of suet in water. Reserve the stock.

Take the stock in which the beef and the suet were cooked and add apples (cored and sliced). Bring to a boil for about 1 hour, or until the apples are cooked. Add everything else and mix well. At the last moment, when the mixture is still hot, add 1 quart applejack and seal hot in mason jars at once.

Baked Apples in Cider

Remove cores of 6 good-sized apples. Plug up the bottom of each and cut out V-shape at top. Insert into the top about 1 tablespoon of cinnamon Imperials (the little red-hot candies) and 1 tablespoon maple syrup. Place the apples in a dish and pour around the apples about 2½ cups hard cider. Bake at 350°, basting occasionally with the hot cider, until tender. Grate nutmeg on apples, and if you like, top off with whipped cream or ice cream.

Cider Applesauce

Applesauce is usually made by cooking apple slices slowly in water, with sugar and spices added for flavor. Applesauce will taste differently if you use cider instead of water.

Cider Apple Butter

8 LBS. APPLES
4 QUARTS SWEET CIDER
3 LBS. SUGAR

1 TEASPOON CLOVES
1 TEASPOON CINNAMON

The apples are pared, cored, and sliced, and then cooked slowly in the cider. When this is cooked enough, sugar is slowly added, along with the spices. Keep cooking and stirring the sauce until the mixture is no longer watery but thick. Good apple butter should be a dark color and be thick enough to cling to a knife.

Maine Apple Butter

Cook 8 lbs. apples, which have been cored and sliced but still have skins, in a dish of 4 quarts hard cider. Stir so it won't burn. Then strain and add 3 lbs. brown or maple sugar, 1 teaspoon each ground cloves and cinnamon. Stir and cook until the mixture is thick.

Cider Jelly

Take 4 cups hard cider and into it mix 1 cup water, ½ cup lemon juice, and 1 cup sugar. Dissolve 3 envelopes of unflavored gelatin in 1½ cups water and add this to the cider mixture when it is warm. Stir and bring to a boil until blended. Remove from stove and add beaten whites of 2 eggs. Stir and let cool in a mold to be put in refrigerator.

Sweet Cider Jelly

Into a saucepan place 4 cups sweet cider, 7½ cups sugar, 1 teaspoon cinnamon, and ½ teaspoon cloves. Boil. When boiling, add 1 bottle of Certo, stirring all the time. Boil for another minute. Then take off heat, and skim. Let cool and place in glasses for sealing.

Vermont Cider Jelly

Empty 1 envelope of unflavored gelatin into enough sweet cider to dissolve it. Take 2 more cups of cider and add the juice of half a lemon, with a pinch of salt and 1 tablespoon sugar. Add the gelatin to mixture and dissolve. Now pour this into a mold and the mixture will form jelly. Keep in cold place.

Cider in Aspic

2½ CUPS SWEET CIDER
2 TABLESPOONS GELATIN
1 CUP SLICED APPLES
SALT TO TASTE

½ CUP CHOPPED NUTS
½ CUP CHOPPED CELERY
SOME GRATED PARSLEY

Bring 1¼ cups cider to a boil and to this add gelatin, which has been dissolved in another 1¼ cups cold cider. Stir all the while. When it is dissolved, cool off in refrigerator. Just before the mixture starts to solidify, add everything else. Place in a mold to form.

Cider Apple Soup

3 CUPS WATER
½ CUP BROWN SUGAR
SALT
ABOUT 6 WINTER APPLES
1 CINNAMON STICK
1 LEMON ·

½ CUP BREAD CRUMBS
2 CUPS HARD CIDER
4 TABLESPOONS LEMON JUICE
3 TABLESPOONS APPLE JELLY
CINNAMON OR NUTMEG

Put water, sugar, and a pinch of salt into a pan and cook to boiling point. Add apples, which have been peeled, cored, and sliced, and cinnamon stick, sliced rind of the lemon, and bread crumbs. Let cook until apples are tender. Then remove cinnamon stick and lemon rind, and strain. Turn the strained mixture into a saucepan. Add cider, and 4 tablespoons lemon juice, and jelly. Let simmer until it is all dissolved. Serve with some grated cinnamon or nutmeg on top. Can be served hot or cold.

Sweet Cider Soup

3 CUPS SWEET CIDER
1 CUP WATER
2 TABLESPOONS FLOUR
1 STICK CINNAMON

SUGAR AND SALT
2 CUPS SCALDED MILK
2 EGG YOLKS, BEATEN

Bring the cider to a boil in a saucepan. Mix flour in water until it is a smooth paste. Pour this into the boiling cider, stirring very fast. While stirring, add cinnamon and cook a few minutes. Remove stick. Add a pinch of salt and a little sugar. Now add the scalding-hot milk and top with the beaten egg yolks.

Herb Cider Soup

1 CUP WATER
2 TABLESPOONS FLOUR
3 CUPS SWEET CIDER
½ TEASPOON BASIL

1 CINNAMON STICK
2 CUPS SCALDED MILK
2 BEATEN EGG YOLKS
1 TEASPOON SUGAR AND SALT

Make a smooth mixture of water and flour. Pour this slowly into the cider, which has been made to boil. Stir fast, then add basil and cinnamon stick and cook 8 minutes. Remove cinnamon stick. Add hot milk but do not boil this mixture. Pour all this into a dish which has the beaten egg yolks in it, and add sugar and a pinch of salt.

Dried-Apple Pie with Cider

½ LB. DRIED APPLES
3 CUPS HARD CIDER
DASH OF GRATED NUTMEG
½ TEASPOON CINNAMON

½ CUP MAPLE SUGAR
SMALL PIECES OF BUTTER
PIE SHELL AND CRUST

Add dried apples to cider and cook until apples are soft. Mix the spices into the sugar. Add to apples and cook 10 minutes more. Put small dabs of butter on the pie shell. Pour the mixture into pie shell. Cover with lattice-top crust. Bake at 400° until done.

Cold Pea Soup

Take what pea soup you have and mix it with an equal amount of sweet cider. Now stir in 1 cup dry sherry and cool. When this mixture is cold, it is ready to serve with a topping of heavy beaten cream, to which you add some minced chives. A couple table-spoons of this topping are laid on each serving of the cold soup.

Apple Pie

First make a baked shell, using stone-ground wheat meal and white flour in equal amounts for a flaky crust. Then take 2 cups sliced apples and add ½ teaspoon each of ground cinnamon and nutmeg and 1 cup maple or brown sugar. Cook. When done, grate orange rind on top to taste. Cool and then mix 1 package of gelatin into 1½ cups of sweet cider. Add this. Chop some almonds and add for flavor. Pour into baked crust and chill in refrigerator. Serve.

Salad Dressing with Cider

For a piquant and different topping for fruit salad, take 3 tablespoons sweet cider and mix into it 1 teaspoon lemon juice. Then blend all with some mayonnaise.

Sweet Cider Sauce for Ham

If you are using a Vermont ham, this has only to be baked. A Southern ham has to be soaked overnight in water and then boiled before it's ready to be baked. The cider sauce is made of 3 cups sweet cider, ¾ cup boiling water, 3 tablespoons sugar syrup, and a large sliced onion. Boil all of this until it is a good blend. Strain, then pour over ham and leave to bake. Time of baking depends upon the kind of ham. A Vermont cob-smoked ham usually stays in the oven at 350° for 1 hour for every 10 lbs. of weight.

Pudding Sauce of Cider

1 TABLESPOON BUTTER
3/4 TABLESPOON FLOUR
1½ CUPS SWEET CIDER
2 TABLESPOONS BROWN SUGAR

1 TEASPOON GROUND CINNAMON
1/4 TEASPOON GROUND CLOVES

Melt the butter and blend in the flour. Add the cider and sugar, stirring all the while. Then add spices. Boil carefully for a few minutes and serve. Can be used hot or cold.

Hard Cider Sauce for Hams

2 TABLESPOONS HARD CIDER
2 TABLESPOONS BUTTER
2 TABLESPOONS WORCESTER-
    SHIRE SAUCE

1 TEASPOON DRY MUSTARD
1 SMALL CAN TOMATO PASTE

Mix everything in a saucepan and bring to a boil, then cool.

Sauce for Baked Lamb

Blend together 1 cup beef boullion, 1 cup sweet cider, and 1 large onion cut into very small pieces. Add a pinch of sugar, a teaspoon of powdered ginger, and 4 pinches of rosemary. Use for basting when lamb is cooking.

Meat Sauce

1/4 CUP MAPLE SUGAR
1/4 CUP WHITE SUGAR
1/2 TEASPOON SALT
1 TABLESPOON FLOUR

2 CUPS SWEET CIDER
1/2 CUP RAISINS
GOOD HANDFUL OF CRUSHED
    ALMONDS

Put into a saucepan the sugar, salt, and flour mixed together. Add the cider and blend, cooking slowly while stirring. Do this long enough for the mixture to become thick. As soon as it starts to boil, turn down the heat. Stir and simmer for a few minutes. At this point add the raisins and almonds. Heat the sauce over a low flame for a few minutes, and it is ready for use on meat.

Cider Cake Sauce

1 CUP CONFECTIONERS' SUGAR
4 TABLESPOONS BUTTER
1/4 CUP SWEET CIDER

2 EGG YOLKS
1/2 CUP EVAPORATED MILK
2 EGG WHITES

Blend sugar and butter into light paste, then beat into this the cider. When egg yolks are beaten, add and mix. Now beat and add the milk and simmer while stirring. (It is better and safer to use a double boiler.) After egg whites are slowly beaten, add the mixture to them. This sauce is good on hot breads as a dessert.

Wild-Game Sauce

1/2 LB. BUTTER
2 TABLESPOONS FLOUR
1 CUP HARD CIDER
SALT AND PEPPER

1 TEASPOON CELERY SALT
1 TABLESPOON WORCESTER-
   SHIRE SAUCE
2 TABLESPOONS SHERRY

Prepare a gravy by thoroughly blending the butter, flour, and cider. Add freshly ground pepper and salt to taste. Then add the celery salt. Heat slowly. After cooking, add Worcestershire and sherry. This will tame any wild game.

Cider and Cheese Sauce

4 TABLESPOONS FLOUR
1 TEASPOON DRY MUSTARD
1 PINT SWEET CIDER

8 OZ. GRATED VERMONT
   CHEESE

Mix the flour, mustard, and cider into a smooth paste. Put this in skillet. Stir and cook until it boils, then simmer for 5 minutes. Take the mixture off the stove and add grated cheese. Stir until cheese has melted into the mixture. Serve on toast or corn bread.

Hard Cider Sauce for Leftovers

Take 3 tablespoons each of chopped onion, celery, butter, and white flour. Cook the onion and celery in the butter for 3 minutes, then add the flour and 1 teaspoon mustard. Cook for a minute and add 1 cup hard cider. Simmer while you salt and pepper to taste. When the mixture gets thick, it is ready to use on any kind of meat loaf or leftovers.

Cider Basting for Turkey

We have used this to baste a whole turkey or a turkey breast when baking and also to moisten turkey stuffing. Warm ½ cup butter in a pan. Add 1 cup hard cider, 1 cup orange juice, and ½ cup lemon juice, all flavored with a bit of crushed basil. Cook over low heat until well dissolved.

Apple Bread

⅞ CUP OIL	1 TABLESPOON ORANGE RIND
1 CUP SUGAR	1 CUP RAISINS
2 EGGS, BEATEN	4 CUPS WALNUTS
3 CUPS WHOLEGRAIN FLOUR	3 CUPS CHOPPED APPLES
2 TEASPOONS BAKING POWDER	½ CUP SWEET CIDER
½ TEASPOON SALT	

Blend the oil and sugar into a smooth cream. Add well-beaten eggs. In a separate bowl, mix the flour, baking powder, and salt. Add this to the cream mix. After mixing together, add the remaining ingredients and stir into smooth, well-kneaded dough. If the dough seems too dry, add some cider. It should neither stick to hands nor crumble. Bake in a pan like a johnnycake at 350° for 45 minutes.

Manual apple crusher used on farms from about 1880 to 1910

RECIPES FROM MARTINELLI'S

The following cider recipes were supplied by Stephen Martinelli, whose California firm makes Apple Cider, Apple Juice, Natural Apple Juice, Old-Fashioned Hard Cider, Sparkling Cider, and Sparkling Apple Juice. The slogan of this 115-year-old cider firm is "Drink Your Apple a Day," which should apply to all cider and cider products and perhaps should be the subtitle of this book.

Beverages

Nature's Instant Breakfast

1 BANANA
1 EGG

1 CUP (OR MORE) CHILLED
APPLE JUICE

Mix for a few seconds in an electric blender, and it's ready to drink. Flavor can be varied by using natural apple juice or by blending the apple juice fifty-fifty with some other juice (grape, cranberry, prune, etc.). Also, a tablespoon of gelatin may be substituted for the egg.

Hot Spiced Cider

1 QUART CIDER
12 WHOLE CLOVES
8 INCHES OF STICK CINNAMON

1/4 TEASPOON POWDERED
ALLSPICE

Add spices to cider and bring to boiling point. Remove from heat and let stand for an hour or more. When ready to serve, reheat. Remove the whole spices. May also be served chilled.

Frosty Apple Drink

1 PINT VANILLA ICE CREAM
1 QUART CHILLED CIDER
1/2 TEASPOON NUTMEG

4–6 SCOOPS VANILLA ICE
   CREAM
FRESHLY GROUND NUTMEG

Allow a pint of ice cream to stand at room temperature until fairly soft. Put in mixer or blender and beat. Add cider gradually and beat until well blended and frothy. Stir in nutmeg. Pour into tall glasses or mugs and top each serving with a scoop of vanilla ice cream. Sprinkle with freshly ground nutmeg.

Halloween Punkin' Punch Bowl

1 HOLLOW PUMPKIN
MARSHMALLOWS
DOUGHNUTS

JELLY BEANS
1 GALLON CIDER
APPLES

Stick marshmallows on toothpicks to make pumpkin's mouth and nose. Doughnuts with jelly-bean centers form the eyes. Hang other doughnuts on skewers in a semicircle around the top of the pumpkin. When ready to serve, fill with chilled cider. Mugs can be made from hollowed-out apples, which are later eaten.

Autumn-Leaf Nectar

3 CUPS CIDER
3 CUPS APRICOT NECTAR

3 TABLESPOONS LEMON JUICE
12 WHOLE CLOVES

Combine all ingredients and heat to boiling. Serve in heated mugs. Makes 6 to 8 servings.

Cider Fruit Punch

3/4 CUP SUGAR
4 CUPS WATER
1/2 CUP ORANGE JUICE

1/4 CUP LEMON JUICE
1/4 CUP PINEAPPLE JUICE
2 CUPS CIDER

Combine all ingredients and serve chilled. Great for parties or picnics. Makes about 10 servings.

Holiday Bowl

2 CUPS CIDER   2 QUARTS GINGER ALE
2 CUPS GRAPE JUICE   ICE
2 CUPS GRAPEFRUIT JUICE   FRESH MINT

Combine all ingredients except ginger ale. Pour over block of ice in large punch bowl. Add ginger ale just before serving. Top each punch glass with a sprig of mint.

Apple-Orange Punch

1 QUART CHILLED CIDER   3 CUPS SPARKLING WATER
1 CAN FROZEN CONCENTRATED   ORANGE SLICES
    ORANGE JUICE   MARASCHINO CHERRIES

Mix cider and orange juice concentrate together until orange juice is melted. Just before serving, add sparkling water and pour into punch bowl over ice cubes. Garnish with orange slices and maraschino cherries. Makes 14 4-oz. servings.

Witches' Brew

1 CUP CIDER   2 EGG WHITES
1/2 CUP ORANGE JUICE   1 TEASPOON POWDERED SUGAR
1/4 CUP LEMON JUICE   NUTMEG

Mix with crushed ice in an electric blender until foamy. Pour into small glasses and top with nutmeg.

Happy Apple Cocktail

2 CUPS CIDER   1 CUP SPARKLING WATER
1 CUP CRANBERRY JUICE   LIME OR LEMON SLICE

Chill juices and sparkling water. Just before serving, combine, and pour into cocktail glasses. Garnish with lime or lemon slice. Serve immediately. Makes 6 to 8 servings.

Cider Milk Shake

In an electric blender mix together 1 cup chilled cider and enough vanilla ice cream (2 heaping tablespoons or more) for desired thickness.

Cider Julep

4 CUPS CIDER
1 CUP PINEAPPLE JUICE
1 CUP ORANGE JUICE

¼ CUP LEMON JUICE
MINT LEAVES

Mix ingredients and serve with ice in tall glasses. Top with fresh mint leaves.

Meat Dishes

Ham Steak

1 CUP CIDER
½ TEASPOON ALLSPICE
¼ TEASPOON PEPPER
½ CUP BROWN SUGAR, FIRMLY
    PACKED

2 TABLESPOONS BUTTER
2 HAM STEAKS, 1 INCH THICK
WHOLE CLOVES

Cook cider, allspice, pepper, and brown sugar to a boil. Reduce heat and cook gently for 20 minutes. Add butter and stir until dissolved. Start oven at 325°. Put ham slices in a shallow baking pan, stud with cloves, and pour cider sauce over the meat. Bake about 1 hour and 15 minutes, basting frequently with the sauce. Serves 6 to 8.

Baked Ham

½ CUP BROWN SUGAR
1 TABLESPOON FLOUR

2 CUPS CIDER
¼ TEASPOON MUSTARD

Cover a clove-studded boiled ham with a mixture of the above ingredients. Baste several times with the liquid during baking.

Baked Ham Polonaise

CLOVES
1 QUART CIDER

1 CUP ORANGE JUICE
BARBADOS MOLASSES

Score a canned ham and dot with cloves. Mix together the cider and orange juice and pour over the ham. Spread evenly with a small amount of molasses. Bake in hot oven (375° to 400°) until brown and thoroughly heated (1 hour). Baste often with cider and orange-juice mixture.

Normandy Pork Chops

6 PORK CHOPS, ¾ INCH THICK
1 TEASPOON SALT
FLOUR
4 APPLES

2 CUPS CRANBERRIES
1 CUP BROWN SUGAR
1½ CUPS CIDER

Sprinkle pork chops with salt. Dredge with flour. Sauté until golden brown. Slice apples thin, mix with cranberries and brown sugar, and put in the bottom of buttered casserole. Lay chops on fruit, add cider. Cook 1½ hours at 350° or until pork is tender. Turn chops during cooking so both sides are flavored with the fruit.

Barbecue Sauce

1 CUP CIDER
¼ CUP CATSUP
1 TEASPOON BROWN SUGAR
1 TEASPOON WORCESTERSHIRE
    SAUCE
1 TEASPOON SALT

1 TEASPOON VINEGAR
¼ TEASPOON DRY MUSTARD
¼ TEASPOON CELERY SEED
¼ CUP CHOPPED ONION
DASH OF PEPPER

Mix ingredients. Use for frequent basting. Perfect for spareribs, chicken, etc.

Pork Skillet Supper

1 TABLESPOON SHORTENING
2 LBS. BONELESS PORK
   SHOULDER OR LEFTOVER
   PORK ROAST, CUT IN
   CUBES
2 CUPS CIDER
2 TABLESPOONS CORNSTARCH
1/2 CUP SUGAR
1/4 CUP VINEGAR

1 TABLESPOON SOY SAUCE
1/2 CUP THIN-SLICED ONION
3/4 CUP GREEN-PEPPER STRIPS
2 TABLESPOONS DICED
   PIMENTO
2 TABLESPOONS CHOPPED
   CANDIED GINGER
   (OPTIONAL)

Brown pork thoroughly in hot shortening. Drain off drippings. Add cider and bring mixture to a boil. Reduce heat and cook gently for 1 hour, or until pork is fork-tender. Mix the cornstarch and sugar in a small saucepan. Add vinegar and 1 cup cider liquid from cooked pork. Mix well. Cook gently for 3 minutes. Add soy sauce to mixture; mix with pork in skillet. Cover and let stand for 15 minutes to blend flavors. Add onion, green pepper, and pimento to pork and cook for 3 minutes. Add ginger. Serve with rice.

Cider Pot Roast

1 1/2 CUPS CIDER
1 TABLESPOON BROWN SUGAR
2 TEASPOONS SALT
1/4 TEASPOON CINNAMON
1/4 TEASPOON GINGER

2 WHOLE CLOVES
3- TO 4-LB. CHUCK POT ROAST
   OF BEEF
FLOUR

Mix marinade of cider, sugar, and spices. Pour over a 3- to 4-lb. chuck pot roast of beef, and let stand in refrigerator 24 hours. Remove from marinade; sprinkle with flour. Brown in hot fat in a Dutch oven. Turn heat low, add marinade to meat, and cover closely. Simmer for 3 hours. Thicken gravy if desired.

Desserts

Apple-Cider Pie

1½ CUPS CIDER
2 TABLESPOONS RED CINNAMON
    CANDIES
1 PACKAGE LEMON-FLAVORED
    GELATIN

2 MEDIUM-LARGE APPLES,
    PARED
1 CUP HEAVY CREAM,
    WHIPPED
9-INCH BAKED PIE SHELL

Heat ¾ cup cider with the cinnamon candies added. When candy has melted, add gelatin and stir until dissolved. Stir in rest of cider. Chill until nearly set. Then beat until frothy. Grate pared apples directly into gelatin mixture and fold in whipped cream. Pour into baked pie shell. Chill until firm.

Cider Sherbet

1 TEASPOON GELATIN
2 TABLESPOONS COLD WATER
1¼ CUPS CIDER

¼ CUP SUGAR
¼ CUP LEMON JUICE
1 EGG WHITE

Soak gelatin in cold water. Heat cider and sugar to boiling point. Dissolve gelatin in the hot cider and add lemon juice. Place in freezing tray until chilled and thick. Then remove from tray and whip until frothy. Fold in stiffly beaten egg white, return to freezing tray, and stir every 15 minutes for the first hour. Serves 4.

Fruit with Cider Sauce

Arrange slightly drained canned fruit cocktail in small dishes. Just before serving, spoon the following piping-hot sauce over the fruit. Simmer 2 tablespoons brown sugar, 8 to 12 whole cloves, 2 slices of lemon (cut ¼ inch thick), and 1¼ cups of cider for 10 minutes. Mix 2 tablespoons cornstarch and a dash of salt with ¼ cup cider. Stir into hot mixture. Boil for 3 minutes. This makes 1 to 1⅓ cups of flavorful sauce.

Cider Syrup

1 QUART CIDER   2½ CUPS SUGAR

Boil cider for 25 minutes. Add sugar. Bring again to full boil for 3 minutes for medium syrup or 5 minutes for heavy syrup. Yield: approximately 1½ pints. For cinnamon cider syrup, add 1 tablespoon cinnamon drops with the sugar and proceed as above. Use medium cider syrup as a table syrup, and heavy cider syrup for ice-cream sundaes and sodas.

Apple Butter

10 CUPS SLICED, PEELED APPLES   ½ TEASPOON SALT
1 TABLESPOON CINNAMON   10 CUPS SUGAR
2 TEASPOONS CLOVES   ½ CUP CIDER
1 TEASPOON NUTMEG   3 TABLESPOONS LEMON JUICE

Mix ingredients and let stand 10 minutes. Cook slowly, stirring frequently, until mixture becomes very soft. This will take about 50 minutes. Pour into sterilized jars and seal immediately.

Apple Marmalade

8 CUPS SLICED, PEELED APPLES   ¼ TEASPOON NUTMEG
7 CUPS SUGAR   ¼ TEASPOON SALT
1 TABLESPOON CINNAMON   4 TABLESPOONS LEMON JUICE
1 TEASPOON CLOVES   2 CUPS CIDER

Mix ingredients, cook slowly, and stir frequently until mixture thickens. It will take an hour of slow cooking. Pour into sterilized jars and seal immediately.

Apples in Cider Sauce

1½ CUPS CIDER   6–8 TART APPLES
¾ CUP BROWN SUGAR

Make light syrup of cider and sugar. When this boils, drop peeled, cored, whole apples into syrup. Cook covered for first 10 minutes, turning from time to time. Cook until apples are tender but not too soft. Cool both apples and rest of syrup and then pour syrup over apples to glaze them. Best when served with pork, lamb, or fowl.

Apple-Cheese Mold

1-QUART RING MOLD OR   ½ CUP DICED CELERY
   6 INDIVIDUAL MOLDS   1 CUP SHREDDED CHEDDAR
1 TABLESPOON (1 ENVELOPE)   CHEESE
   UNFLAVORED GELATIN   1 TEASPOON GRATED ONION
2 CUPS APPLE JUICE   ½ CUP SHREDDED CABBAGE
½ CUP DAIRY SOUR CREAM   ½ CUP CHOPPED, UNPEELED
¾ TEASPOON SALT   RED APPLE
½ CUP DICED CUCUMBER

Soften gelatin in ½ cup juice. Heat remaining 1½ cups apple juice to boiling and stir into softened gelatin until dissolved. Chill until mixture begins to set. Then fold in sour cream, salt, cucumber, celery, cheddar cheese, onion, cabbage, and apple. Pour into a 1-quart mold or individual molds, which have been rinsed in cold water. Chill until firm. Unmold on dark greens. Garnish with apple slices that have been dipped in fruit juice to prevent discoloring.

RECIPES FROM BULMER'S

The following recipes come from Bulmer's, the famous English cider-making establishment, who are pioneers in using cider in cooking. Their Strongbow Cider is what we call hard cider; their dry cider is a fermented, bottled cider with an alcoholic content, and their Woodpecker Cider is a sweet, bottled cider, sparkling like champagne.

Golden Valley Bananas

½ PINT SPARKLING SWEET
    CIDER
JUICE OF ½ LARGE LEMON
1 OZ. GRANULATED SUGAR

4 BANANAS
¼ PINT HEAVY CREAM
TOASTED ALMONDS

Pour cider into a shallow pan with a wide base, add lemon juice and sugar, and boil for 5 minutes. Peel bananas, cut into halves across, and split lengthwise. Put into the hot cider, cover with lid, and simmer for 3 minutes. Put bananas into serving dish, add the juice, and leave to cool. Chill in the refrigerator for 20 minutes before serving. Decorate with whipped cream (which can be colored pink) and sprinkle with toasted almonds. Serves 4.

Cider Chicken

4 CHICKEN QUARTERS
BUTTER AND OIL
1 SMALL ONION, CHOPPED
1 TABLESPOON FLOUR
SALT AND PEPPER
1/2 LEVEL TEASPOON
    GROUND GINGER

1 LEVEL TEASPOON PAPRIKA
3/4 PINT HARD CIDER
1 TABLESPOON TOMATO
    PURÉE
1/4 TEASPOON SUGAR
1 TABLESPOON CHOPPED
    PARSLEY

Fry the chicken in oil and butter until browned. Remove, and fry the onion until soft. Work in flour, salt and pepper, ginger, and paprika. Add the cider to make a sauce, and stir in the tomato purée, sugar, and parsley. Return chicken to the pan, baste well, cover, and simmer for 20 minutes or cook in oven for 30 minutes at 325°. Arrange a border of mashed potatoes on a serving dish. Put chicken in the center and pour the sauce over. Serves 4.

Ham and Cheese

2 OZ. BUTTER
2 OZ. FLOUR
SALT AND PEPPER
1/2 TEASPOON MUSTARD

1 PINT HARD CIDER
8 OZ. CHEDDAR CHEESE
8 OZ. COOKED HAM

Topping:

2 OZ. FRESH BREAD CRUMBS
3 OZ. GRATED CHEESE

1 OZ. CHOPPED WALNUTS

Make a smooth sauce from the butter, flour, salt, pepper, mustard, and cider. Cook for a few minutes. Remove from heat and stir in the cheese and then the ham, both cut into small cubes. Pour into a large shallow dish or four individual ones. Mix the bread crumbs, 2 ozs. of the cheese, and the walnuts, and spread over the top. Sprinkle with the rest of the cheese. Brown under hot grill. This dish can be prepared in advance and warmed in the oven for 10–15 minutes. Serves 4.

Sweet Coppin' Apples

½ PINT SPARKLING SWEET   1 LB. DESSERT APPLES
    CIDER   2 OZ. BROWN SUGAR

Pour the cider into a pan and bring to boiling point. Add the apples, peeled, cored, and cut into eighths. Cook gently until the apples are tender but retain their shape. Drain and put into an ovenproof dish. Sprinkle with the sugar. Boil the cider until reduced to 2–3 tablespoons. Then pour over the sugar. Put under a hot grill to brown the top. Serves 4.

Cider Cod

1 LB. COD FILLETS   SALT AND PEPPER
8 MEDIUM MUSHROOMS   1 OZ. BUTTER
2 LARGE TOMATOES, HALVED 1 OZ. FLOUR
½ PINT HARD CIDER   2–3 OZ. GRATED CHEESE

Cut the cod into four pieces and arrange in a greased ovenproof dish with mushrooms and tomatoes. Pour cider slowly over the ingredients and season with salt and pepper. Bake for 15 minutes in a fairly hot oven. Meanwhile, melt butter, add the flour, and cook for a few minutes. Add liquid from the fish, bring to a boil, and cook gently for a few minutes. Pour this sauce over the fish, and if desired, pipe creamed potatoes around the edge of the dish. Sprinkle with the grated cheese and brown under a hot grill.

BOILED CIDER

Boiled cider is, I believe, a unique New England concoction. I have never heard of it outside this part of the world, nor do I find references to it in cookbooks other than those of New England. Yet in Vermont it has a long and rich tradition.

What is it?

Boiled cider is the syrup of cider. Boiled cider is to sweet cider what maple syrup is to sweet sap. When sweet cider is boiled down to the right consistency, you get a dark syrup of about the same thickness as maple syrup.

Its use in cooking and flavoring is well known in Vermont. When I was a boy and visited my grandparents on a northern Vermont farm, where my grandfather had a good apple orchard and made good cider, my grandmother made a dish the memory of which even today makes my mouth water. It was called dried-apple boiled-cider pie. In Vermont farmhouses in the early days, apples were peeled, cored and quartered, and then strung on twine string. The long strings of apples would be tied to wood poles, which hung from the kitchen ceiling by forged-iron hooks. Kept there for long winter weeks with the kitchen fire going, the slices of apple dried and darkened and when used in pies gave a flavor that no fresh apples ever did or could. (Of course, you had to soak the slices overnight before you made the pie.) The principal reason for the superb taste of my grandmother's pie was the boiled cider that she made on the kitchen stove. It was tangy, pungent, rich, tart, and wonderful. I suspect also that the generous amounts of soft maple sugar she used with the apples did not hurt the pie any. Ever since those far-off days, all apple pies I have eaten since have tasted insipid.

In the last several decades, boiled cider in Vermont (and I am sure this is even more so outside New England) has been known only to the few old-timers with a memory. And had it not been for one man, I fear this syrup would have been totally forgotten. Certainly there was nothing like it on the market until recent years when one or two other people found a demand for this rare indigenous product and set up its manufacture.

Although I should like to honor this man, who is eighty-five years old as this book is being written, and I'd like to mention his name so he might occupy a well-earned place in the culinary records of Vermont, I dare not. I value his privacy, his independence, and his way of life too much. You will see why.

He lives in the hills in an old farmhouse that has received no "improvements" since he was born in it. The low, slant-roof, clapboarded house, one story high and with a central chimney, clings to the hill as if it grew there. It is a fine example of what we call "continuous architecture." The woodshed is hitched to the house, the sled and wagon shed to the woodshed, and the barn to the sled and wagon shed, and finally the cider mill to the barn. This style was designed not for looks but for necessity. You could get to the wood, the sleds, and the cows and horses without having to go outdoors and shovel snow.

My friend's ancient structure was built in 1798. As soon as an apple orchard could be started and apples grown, the cider mill was erected. The mill was originally run by water power from the brook down from the house. Later, when the present occupant took over some sixty years ago, the cider mill was moved up to the barn and there run first by gasoline engine and later by electric motor.

This strong, hearty, lively old man lives alone. If he is not an image of the classic independent character of Ethan Allen and the Green Mountain Boys, I have never seen one. He chooses to live this way. He did have a choice. After graduating from an agricultural college, he could have gone out and farmed the rich lands in the West. Instead, he chose the family homestead and cider.

It is not, however, cider that made him famous, but *boiled* cider and the product of boiled cider, which is cider jelly. All his life he has made from his own cider, in the old-fashioned kitchen, these two unique Vermont products.

I visited him one cool autumn day. The kitchen was so crowded that I could hardly get in and find a chair. In front of the big kitchen fireplace sat an old black iron kitchen range. On two pine kitchen tables with the leaves up sat dozens of bottles of boiled-cider syrup and glass jars of boiled-cider jelly that he had made the day before on the stove. At the third table stood a tall, eighteen-year-old girl busy rolling out dough. After a while he said she was a granddaughter of a friend, visiting him for a spell. After she told me what she was doing and how, she went into the buttery and brought out a boiled-cider pie, cut a piece, and handed it to me on a plate. This is the recipe she gave me for boiled-cider apple pie without apples:

Blend 3 tablespoons butter and 3 of flour. Gradually add ½ cup hard cider, ½ cup boiled cider, and 1 cup maple syrup. Cook in a double boiler until thick. Cool. Add 1 beaten egg, and 1 cup raisins or currants. Bake with two crusts at 425° for 10 minutes and then at 325° until done.

This was the first boiled-cider pie I had eaten for many years. But it was not the last.

Actually, it was not the traditional boiled-cider apple pie my grandmother used to make. Hers were made of dried apples flavored with boiled-cider syrup. I have included several recipes for both kinds; one without apples and one with apples flavored with boiled cider. It is no longer possible, except in the Dutch markets of Lancaster County, Pennsylvania, to buy dried apples, so the cook who wishes to capture that rare flavor of my grandmother's time will have to dry her own. That failing, passably good pies can be made with fresh sliced (or canned) apples, and the boiled-cider syrup.

Our friend in the farmhouse then told me some of the ways boiled cider was used in his youth. One drink he remembers was called "jelly water." Served with chunks of ice from the icehouse in summer to hands in the hayfield, it was made of boiled-cider jelly dissolved in water laced with powdered ginger! It could also be made of boiled-cider syrup.

In addition, of course, to the classic boiled-cider pie, our friend mentioned uses in making mincemeat and baked apples, and claimed that boiled cider was very good on pancakes. His mother used to pour it on Indian pudding and sweet potatoes, make apple butter with it, and candy too. When they made brine for pickling ham, boiled cider was one ingredient.

Before I give any recipes for boiled-cider pie, I will suggest that the crust be made the old-fashioned way, with stone-ground wholegrain flour.

This can be done as follows:

Pastry or Pie Crust*

1½ CUPS STONE-GROUND
    WHEAT PASTRY FLOUR
¾ TEASPOON SALT
½ TEASPOON BAKING POWDER

½ CUP (LESS 1 TABLESPOON)
    SHORTENING
⅓ CUP COLD WATER

Measure the 1½ cups flour, add salt and baking powder, and sift into mixing bowl. Blend in shortening with a pastry cutter. The mixture should hold together when pinched between fingertips. If it does not, add more shortening. Dampen with cold water from the tap. Do not use ice water. Mix to a dough. Sift a small amount of wheat flour over a pastry cloth, just barely covering the cloth. Cut off enough dough to line a pie plate, and roll out on cloth. Turn the pastry over frequently to keep from sticking. Roll as thin as possible and line the pie plate. Fill with any desired pie filling. Roll out the upper crust in the same manner as the lower. Dampen the rim of the under crust with more cold water and press upper crust into place with a fork dipped in the wheat flour. Cut slits in upper crust before placing on pie. Trim both crusts and bake at 400° for 30 minutes. Bake longer if the filling requires it.

Boiled-Cider Pie, without Apples

1 CUP SUGAR
4 TABLESPOONS BOILED CIDER
4 TABLESPOONS WATER

2 EGGS
2 TABLESPOONS FLOUR
1 TEASPOON VANILLA (SCANT)

Boil sugar, cider, and water. Beat eggs, flour, and stir into syrup. Add vanilla. Bake in two crusts. Makes an 8-inch pie.

* From *Cooking with Wholegrains,* by Mildred Ellen Orton.

Boiled-Cider Pie, with Cream

1 EGG, BEATEN   1 TABLESPOON FLOUR
1 CUP SUGAR   1/4 TEASPOON SALT
1/2 CUP BOILED CIDER
3/4 CUP CREAM (LIGHT OR
    HEAVY)

Mix and bake in two crusts in 8-inch pie plate.

Boiled-Cider Pie, with Raisins

1/2 CUP BUTTER   1 1/2 CUPS SUGAR
3 TABLESPOONS FLOUR   1 EGG, BEATEN
1 CUP HOT WATER   1/2 CUP CHOPPED RAISINS
1/2 CUP BOILED CIDER

Cream butter and flour. Add and cook with other ingredients
except raisins, which are added when mixture is taken from the
stove. Use two crusts. Makes a 9-inch generous pie.

Maine Boiled-Cider Pie, without Apples

1 CUP MAPLE SUGAR   1/2 CUP BOILED CIDER
1/3 CUP FLOUR   1 CUP HOT WATER
1 EGG, BEATEN   PASTRY FOR CRUSTS

Mix the sugar and flour with the beaten egg. Blend in the
boiled cider and then the hot water to create the filling. Pour this
into a pie plate lined with crust. With more crust make lattice
top. Bake in 435° oven for 10 minutes, then at 325° for half an
hour.

Boiled-Cider Pie, with Apples

PASTRY FOR A TWO-CRUST
    9-INCH PIE
1 CUP SUGAR
3 TABLESPOONS CORNSTARCH
SALT TO TASTE

½ CUP BOILED CIDER
1½ CUPS BOILING WATER
1 EGG, BEATEN
1 TABLESPOON MELTED BUTTER
2 CUPS SLICED APPLES

Fit bottom crust into a pan. Combine the sugar, cornstarch, and salt in a bowl. Add the boiled cider and water and mix. Then add the egg and butter. Lay out apples on the crust in pan and add the filling. Place the top crust where it belongs and crimp it tight. Slash cuts in top crust and bake in oven 425° for 40 minutes or until done.

Miss Butters's Vermont Recipes

The following boiled-cider recipes by Miss Marion Butters of Brookfield, Vermont, whose talent as a cook is well known in that region of the Green Mountains, were contributed by Mrs. Robert Frick.

Boiled-Cider Pie (Latticed)

10 TABLESPOONS BOILED CIDER   1½ CUPS SUGAR
6 TABLESPOONS FLOUR   1 EGG, BEATEN
12 TABLESPOONS WATER

Combine cider, flour, water, and sugar and cook until mixture thickens. Cool and add 1 beaten egg. Use two crusts but lattice the top one for 8-inch pie plate.

Open-Top Boiled-Cider Pie, without Apples

⅓ CUP MAPLE SUGAR   ¼ CUP RAISINS
½ CUP BOILED CIDER   ½ TEASPOON GRATED NUTMEG
2 EGGS, BEATEN   PIE CRUST
1 TEASPOON BUTTER   MERINGUE

Cook maple sugar in the boiled-cider syrup until the sugar is dissolved, then slowly put in the beaten eggs and stir until it becomes a thick mixture. Now add butter, raisins, and spice. Turn this mixture into a baking pie pan lined with crust. Bake for 10 minutes at 450° and then at 325° for half an hour. When taken from oven, top with a white meringue made of egg whites and confectioners' sugar. Then brown in oven.

Boiled-Cider Pie

Dissolve ⅓ cup maple sugar in ⅓ cup boiled cider. Add 2 eggs, stirring until thickened. Add ½ teaspoon nutmeg, 1 teaspoon butter, and ½ cup chopped raisins. Pour into baked pie shell. Cover with meringue and brown. Makes a 9-inch pie.

Boiled-Cider Pie, without Apples

1 CUP BROWN SUGAR	½ CUP BOILED CIDER
YOLKS OF 2 EGGS	¼ TEASPOON CINNAMON
½ CUP BREAD CRUMBS	¼ TEASPOON CLOVES

Mix everything together and place in prepared pie crust with no top. Bake until done. You can serve with whipped cream.

Boiled-Cider Sweet Applesauce

Core, peel, and quarter 10 Tolman sweet apples. Add 1 cup boiled cider and cook until tender. Apples will hold their shape. The taste improves the longer they stand. Will keep in jars without sealing.

Boiled-Cider Sauce
(for Steamed Pudding)

⅓ CUP BUTTER   ½ CUP BOILING WATER
1 CUP SUGAR   4 TABLESPOONS BOILED CIDER
2 TABLESPOONS CORNSTARCH

Blend butter, sugar, and cornstarch to a cream. Add ½ cup boiling water. Stir constantly until it thickens. Let cook in double boiler for 20 minutes. Before serving, add 4 tablespoons boiled cider.

Boiled-Cider Hard Sauce*

2 TABLESPOONS BUTTER   BOILED CIDER
1 CUP CONFECTIONERS' SUGAR

Blend the butter and sugar until crumbly. Then add just enough boiled cider to dampen the sugar. Beat until smooth, then place in the refrigerator until hard.

Boiled-Cider Applesauce

3 QUARTS SWEET APPLES   1 CUP MAPLE SUGAR
2 CUPS BOILED CIDER   WATER

Peel, core, and quarter apples. Then place them in earthenware dish with cover. Pour in the cider and the maple sugar (dissolved in water, maple syrup can be used). Cover tightly and bake slowly for several hours until soft and a dark red color.

---

* From *Cooking with Wholegrains* by Ellen Orton.

Kempton's Vermont Recipes

The following recipes for using Vermont boiled cider were furnished by James G. Kempton of Northfield, Vermont. Mr. Kempton makes boiled cider. He obtained these recipes over the years from old-time Vermont cooks. They are still used in northern Vermont.

Boiled-Cider Pie

1 CUP BOILED CIDER
3 EGGS, SEPARATED
1 CUP SUGAR
1 CUP MILK

1½ TABLESPOONS FLOUR
2 TABLESPOONS MELTED
    BUTTER

Line a large pie plate with pastry having a fluted edge. Combine cider, egg yolks, sugar, milk, flour, and melted butter. Fold in beaten egg whites last. Pour into pastry-lined pie plate. Bake at 450° for 10 minutes to set the rim, then reduce heat to 325° for 30 minutes.

Boiled-Cider Pie
(Two Crusts)

YOLKS OF 2 EGGS
1 CUP SUGAR
½ CUP BOILED CIDER
2 VERMONT CRACKERS ROLLED
    FINE

¼ TEASPOON CINNAMON
½ TEASPOON CLOVES

Beat yolks, add other ingredients. Make and bake like any two-crust pie.

5

Some Final Observations

ON CIDER VINEGAR

*A*s we have mentioned before, there are two ways to make commercial cider vinegar: the slow way in barrels which takes three years; and the quick way, with a vinegar generator, which takes three days.

At home you can make cider vinegar in a simple way. Let sweet cider stand at room temperature of over 70° in its gallon jug with the screw top off for five weeks or more. Nature will turn it into vinegar.

A quicker way is to add some "mother" to a container of sweet cider. When the "mother" (bacteria) has done its job (which is to create acetic acid), you will have vinegar and can remove the "mother."

The easiest way, and if you count your time, the cheapest, is to buy good, sound, natural cider vinegar from someone you trust not to have filled it with additives to "preserve" it.

Medical Properties of Apple Cider and Apple-Cider Vinegar

It would be extremely foolhardy and could be dangerous for any writer who is not a medical doctor to go deeply into the subject of cider and cider vinegar as medical panaceas. This I shall avoid. But I could not consider this book complete without mentioning two medical doctors whose works in this field were famous in their time.

The first was Dr. Edouard Denis-Dumont, born in France in 1830. He spent his life investigating and conducting clinical experiments with cider as medicine in Normandy, the great cider-producing region of France. In 1883 at Caen, Dr. Denis-Dumont published his famous work, *Medical and Hygienic Properties of Cider and Its Manufacture*. This book was reissued in 1914 at Caen by the Syndicat Général des Cidres and was termed a "monument to the glory of cider." It is of great interest, not only in the long and rich history of cider making, but in the discovery this famous French surgeon made that the people of Normandy were tall, robust, and healthy and exhibited great energy and a strong constitution, a condition he attributed to the properties of cider, which they drank freely. In view of the prejudice that existed in the doctor's lifetime against cider and in favor of wine, his contribution was unique. His treatise of the relation of cider in Normandy to the incidence of gall-bladder disease, kidney stones, gout, dental caries, diabetes, and urinary troubles marks perhaps the first acceptance by a trained scientist of cider as a natural therapeutic agent. Dr. Denis-Dumont's contribution to the history of cider making in France is also notable. His opinion that cider was a salubrious, hygienic, agreeable drink in general, and one exhibiting what he called "prophylactic properties" in particular, is noteworthy.

Five years before Dr. Denis-Dumont's death in 1885, there was born in Vermont a man who was to make cider and cider vinegar nationally known as a medical remedy for many of the troubles of man. This was Dr. DeForest Clinton Jarvis, a graduate of the College of Medicine at the University of Vermont. He began practicing his specialty of ophthalmology and otolaryngology in Barre, Vermont, in 1909. His interest in the natural properties of cider was a hobby but he pursued it throughout his life until it culminated in one of the most fascinating and controversial books written in modern times by a medical man, *Folk Medicine: A Vermont Doctor's Guide to Good Health.*

The theories of Dr. Jarvis were based on a long scientific study of old-time folk remedies, the origins of which lay in Vermont farm life, which he was able to observe at first hand. His application of many such remedies to the cure of human ills was also directed to the prevention of sickness and maintenance of good health by natural means, a subject that is popular today. His theory was applied to the treatment of diseases that ranged all the way from arthritis, kidney trouble (an echo back to Dr. Denis-Dumont), and obesity to hypertension, fatigue, and headaches. This won him national fame and aroused contention among the more orthodox of the medical profession, especially among the government bureaucrats who have undertaken a mission to guard us against our own ideas. The fact that Dr. Jarvis made a major contribution with his theories about the medical use of honey and cider vinegar was a slap in the face to the universal acceptance of the many modern and synthetic miracle drugs. Since most of Dr. Jarvis's ideas were drawn from folk ideas passed down from one generation to another among the farm people of Vermont, many scientists pooh-poohed them. Yet the fact that Dr. Jarvis's ideas had worked for generations, that they were widely applied by thousands of Americans as a result of his publications, could be ignored but not denied.

One of the therapeutic agents Dr. Jarvis made popular was an emulsion of natural Vermont strained honey and natural cider vinegar. From my personal knowledge of and acquaintance with Dr. Jarvis, I know his long record of significant clinical data and success was as impressive as his sincerity and his high standing as a member of the national Academy of Ophthalmology and Otolaryngology, not to mention his editorship of the magazine *Medical World.* And I can tell you from my own experience that when I wake up at three o'clock in the morning and can't go back to sleep I take two or three tablespoons of the famous Jarvis mixture of cider vinegar and honey and I'm back to a sound sleep in no time. Why this is so, I do not know, nor does it matter. I am only one of the many who have benefited from the folk-medicine ideas of Dr. D. C. Jarvis.

Today brochures and publications written by others draw some of their ideas and principles from the pioneer work of this Vermont physician. Once I asked one of my brothers, a practicing physician of thirty years' experience, about the use of honey and vinegar. His reply was comforting. He said he knew of no scientific evidence, in medical publications, that the honey-and-vinegar concoction would do any good. On the other hand, he said, there was certainly no evidence that it would do any harm.

ON COOKING WITH CIDER

Of the making of recipes, as of the making of books, there is no end. Designs for cooking or the concoction of beverages are not holy writ. They are essentially ideas upon which cooks, with ingenuity, can play many themes.

As all students of American history know, housewives in the eighteenth and well into the nineteenth century made up most of their own ways of cooking: rural women had no recipe books. This is why, even though the reader may spend days searching great libraries of early Americana, few early *printed* recipes for the use of cider in cooking will be found.

When books of recipes began to appear, they were made mostly from word-of-mouth cooking methods handed down from mother to daughter. In all such folklore and in all printed recipes of later times for the use of cider, the principles remain essentially the same: cider was used as a flavor to make food taste better.

This is why I hope that American women will not be satisfied with the recipes I have included in this book. Using them as a base on which to build variations, the imaginative cook will make new voyages of discovery and go beyond frontiers of custom to end with the thrill of creation.

Cider, I cannot emphasize too strongly, is not one of but actually is *the one* American drink that has everything. It is pure, natural, and organic. It is the only beverage that a person so inclined can make from the ground to the bottle. A man can plant his own apple orchard, grow his own apples, make his own cider, all without venturing off his home place. And from that achievement, his wife can go further and enjoy the satisfaction of being a pioneer in cooking and making beverages with cider.

Appendix

SUPPLIES FOR MAKING CIDER

*T*o aid the cider maker, we suggest a few sources of supply as of the time of this book's publication in 1973. The list is, naturally, not complete and consists only of firms I have dealt with personally or know by reputation.

One of the most convenient suppliers of general equipment for making wine, cider, and other beverages is Wine-Art of America, with headquarters at 4324 Geary Boulevard, San Francisco, California 94118. In 1973, these people had ninety-five branch shops in the United States and two in Canada, all listed under the firm name Wine-Art, located in California, Colorado, Georgia, Illinois, Indiana, Iowa, Kansas, Kentucky, Maryland, Massachusetts, Michigan, Minnesota, Missouri, Nebraska, New Jersey, New York, North Carolina, Ohio, Oklahoma, Oregon, Pennsylvania, Texas, Tennessee, Virginia, Washington, and Wisconsin. Since changes occur, however, our advice is to write the Wine-Art people in San Francisco and ask for their catalog. You could also request the name and address of the branch nearest you. I list them as one national source I know about and also because their illustrated catalog contains every apparatus that you need for making cider in your own home. They carry everything from oak barrels, corks, and wine yeast to Campden tablets, large presses, and other equipment.

I have examined catalogs of many other supply houses, but since addresses change, my recommendation is to consult the yellow pages of the telephone directory, under the heading *Wine Makers' Supplies*.

For small apparatus and utensils such as the cider press I use in my own home, I refer to *The Voice of the Mountains*, a national mail-order catalog published by The Vermont Country Store, Rockingham, Vermont 05101. Here are also listed stone-ground products, maple syrup, and apple-cider vinegar, to mention only a few. Planned for future issues is a combination cider press and apple grinder in one unit. This may be the most suitable piece of equipment for home or farm use.

Power presses and other motor-driven equipment for those who intend to make larger quantities of cider are manufactured by the Day Equipment Corporation, 1402 East Monroe Street, Goshen, Indiana 46526. Power machines that grind or crush apples into pomace are made by the Buffalo Hammer Mill Corporation of 1245 McKinley Parkway, Buffalo, New York 14218.

Index

acetic acid, 62, 125

Adams, John, 16

additives, *see* chemical agents, fermentation, preservation of cider

alcoholic beverages, consumption of, 17

alcoholic cider, *see* champagne cider, dry cider, English cider, hard cider, sparkling cider

Allen, Ruth Howard, 24

apple butter, 93, 108

apple juice, 28–30, 44, 50, 59, 60–1

apple marmalade, 108

apple products, 46, 61–2

apple wine, 57

applejack, 25

apples: acid content of, 31; classification of, 42–3, 45; baked, 88, 92; growing of in the U.S., 12, 14–15, 43; in history and legend, 7, 15; introduced to America, 15; mixture for cider, 30–1, 40, 44–6; oxidizing of, 33, 67; as sacred fruit, 7; sugar content of, 31, 60; varieties of, 10, 12, 14, 16, 30–1, 44–6; *see also* crab apples, fall apples, summer apples, winter apples

applesauce, 88, 92, 122

Appleseed, Johnny, 15

ascorbic acid, in juice and cider, 21, 29, 50; as preservative, 29, 50, 60

aspic, apples in, 94

barrels, treatment of, 36, 40, 51–2

Barry, P., 14–15

Basselin, Oliver, 9

Beadle, Leigh P., 28

Beecher, Harry Ward, 14

beer, 7, 12, 16

Bergen County, N.J., 24–5

beverages made with cider, 78–86, 101–4; and barley, 83; and bourbon, 80; and brandy, 78–80, 82, 84–6; breakfast drink, 101; and Cu-